MYSTERY OF HANDSHAKE:
THE REST OF MY STORY

An Autobiography
by
Clayton Jennings

Copyright © 1995 by
CLAYTON JENNINGS
& CAROL JENNINGS
P.O. Box 436
Highmore, SD 57345
Phone: 605-852-2001

Library of Congress
Catalog Card No. 95-92505

ISBN 0-9638624-2-1 (Hardcover)
ISBN 0-9638624-3-x (Paperback)

Cover Art:
Handshake by Haley Hemminger
Rope by Lavonne Dyck

Printed in United States of America

PINE HILL PRESS, INC.
Freeman, S. Dak. 57029

Table of Contents

Dedication v
Preface vii

PART I (1913 - 1932)

Chapter 1 Remembering Mother 2
Chapter 2 Remembering Dad 7
Chapter 3 Dad's Ten Commandments for Ted and Me 13
Chapter 4 Partnership 14
Chapter 5 Baseball - 1920 17
Chapter 6 The Day of the Horse 19
Chapter 7 Ristau's Pool Hall 26
Chapter 8 Threshing and Homebrew 28
Chapter 9 Watermelon Mania 30
Chapter 10 Ted Jennings - 440 Yards 32

PART II (1932 - 1946)

Chapter 11 Ed Hartland 36
Chapter 12 Knipplings Hat Brand Ranch 40
Chapter 13 Duff 50
Chapter 14 Sutton Brothers Ranch 54
Chapter 15 Ft. Dodge Serum Company 58
Chapter 16 Jim Magness - The Master Auctioneer 59
Chapter 17 Rawhide 63
Chapter 18 Navy Fighting and Fun 75
Chapter 19 My Golden Horses 86

PART III (1945 - 1964)

Chapter 20 Hyland Angus Ranch 94
Chapter 21 Hyland Angus Ranch Crew 107
Chapter 22 Bull Sales at the Hyland Angus Ranch 111
Chapter 23 Hyland Angus Ranch Champions 117
Chapter 24 Showdown 138
Chapter 25 Walter 143
Chapter 26 J. C. Penney 147
Chapter 27 Wilbur's Feed and Seed Store 153
Chapter 28 Junior Suhn - Commercial Ranch Foreman 156
Chapter 29 I'll Do the Best I Can 162

Chapter 30 The Late 40's and 50's With Doc Cropsey 169
Chapter 31 Rand VanDervoort and Artificial Insemination 173
Chapter 32 From Summer Hay Crew to AI Technician 178
Chapter 33 Bob-Tailed Heifers 184
Chapter 34 Let's Paint the West Black Sale 189
Chapter 35 Frances 191
Chapter 36 June 195
Chapter 37 All American Romance 197
Chapter 38 South American Trip - 1960 205
Chapter 39 International Beef Breeders 217
Chapter 40 600 Purebred Angus Heifers 226
Chapter 41 This Old House 231
Chapter 42 Texas Hunters 235
Chapter 43 Sale of Hyland Angus Ranch News Release 239

PART IV (1964 - 1990)
Chapter 44 My Highmore Home and
                Livestock Handling Facility 244
Chapter 45 A Test of Courage 251
Chapter 46 Caravelle Cattle Company 255
Chapter 47 Spring Storm Catastrophe 260
Chapter 48 Smith Ranch 261
Chapter 49 Who Was Pat Cowan? 266
Chapter 50 Easland Limousin 278
Chapter 51 Harvey Tschetter 283
Chapter 52 Peterson Farms 286
Chapter 53 The Last of 12,000 289

Part V (1990 - 1995)
Chapter 54 My Wife Carol - Her Story 296
Chapter 55 To Laugh Often and Love Much 308
Chapter 56 Everything I Hold Dear 309
Chapter 57 To My Dad 314
Chapter 58 Impressions 315
Chapter 59 What More Do I Need? 316

Dedication

TO MY WIFE CAROL
MY EVERYTHING

Preface

Why another Handshake?

My first book "HANDSHAKE, Code of the West" was so rewarding and gratifying that I felt that you needed to know all the rest about me and I wanted to put it in print.

Every one of you who bought my first book, "HANDSHAKE, Code of the West", have contributed to my present welfare and happiness and made a better and more enjoyable life for me. The many responses from you, the readers, by letter, by telephone and in person, were absolutely beautiful and gave me such a glorious feeling. I just had to tell you the rest of my story. I hope and trust this book "Mystery of Handshake" will give you additional insight into humanity.

During my 82 years of life, I have dealt with most all types of humanity and I have found it most interesting, but not always understandable!

I find that most decisions are influenced by temptation, greed, prosperity, love and hate.

PART I
1913 - 1932

A farm in Boone County, Iowa, was the home for my family, Charles and Mary Jennings, sisters Nadine and Margaret and brother Ted. I was born in 1913 and this farm was my home for the first seven years of my life. In 1920 we moved into Boone, Iowa. Dad had quit farming and was dealing exclusively in cattle and hogs.

We lived in Boone until I was in the fifth grade. Then we moved to Livermore, Iowa, as Dad had the opportunity to take over the hog contract held by his brother, W. O. Jennings, with Wilson Packing Company of Cedar Rapids, Iowa.

While in Livermore Dad's health failed and he was bedridden, so Ted and I became partners in his business at a very early age.

I spent the rest of my youth in Livermore attending school, participating in sports and working with my dad and my brother. Upon graduating from Livermore high school I went to South Dakota to work and live.

Chapter 1

Remembering Mother

My mother, Mary, was an absolutely beautiful woman. She was immaculate in our home and in person. She was kind and gentle and considerate of all people. My sisters, brother and I loved our Mother very much. We wanted at all times to please her and be deserving of her pleasant smile. If Ted or I did something that displeased her, we knew it by her disappointed expression. We would beg for mercy and soon she forgave.

It seems that Mother had the responsibility of disciplining my two older sisters, Nadine and Margaret. My Dad, Charlie, seemed to

Mary Vogler Jennings as a young women

do most of the disciplining of brother Ted and me. But when it came to her home, she made Ted and I toe the mark. This is some discipline that Mother used that I can remember oh-so-well. Ted and I had developed a habit, when we came in from the outdoors for the day and went into our living room, of untying our shoestrings and kicking our shoes off and letting them go in any direction. Mother happened to be in the kitchen one evening when we were quite boisterous and we kicked them off onto the wall and up to the ceiling. Mother heard the resounding noise and knew what we had done. She grabbed Ted by the arm and took him over to where one shoe was and told him to pick it up and then to the other shoe. Then she took him over by one wall and told him to put the shoes, toe-to-toe and heel-to-heel, along the wall, and then told him to sit down, which Ted did! Then Mother took me by the arm and used the same procedure and told me to sit down beside Ted, which I did! Mother stood in front of us and said, "Boys, that's enough of that. How do you expect me to keep a house neat and clean when you boys act like ruffians?" She got her point across, as ever since and even today, I line my shoes up toe-to-toe and heel-to-heel.

Clayton and Ted Jennings - 1914

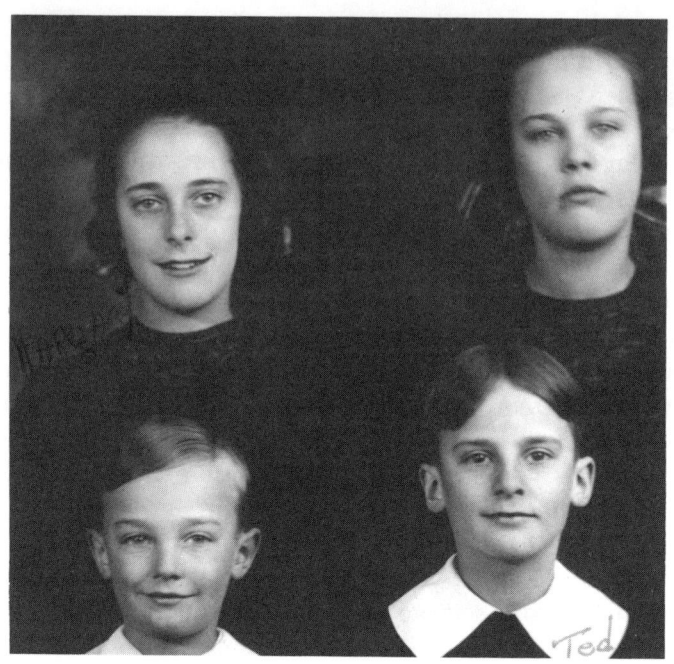
Margaret and Nadine, Ted and Clayton - about 1918

When Ted and I were small, my two sisters had the assignment to care for us when we were outside playing in the barn, feedlot and orchard. The girls had their hands full riding herd on us. We were aggressive and swift. We liked to climb the windmill and on the barn roof. We climbed the trees in the orchard, and had numerous falls, but none were fatal. We were warned every fall not to eat the apples until they were ripe, but when no one was looking we ate the green apples and ended up with a severe belly-ache! Mother would nurse us back to nearly normal in a few hours with a Watkins product that was rated as a cure-all.

Mother was an excellent cook, and no one came by at mealtime without eating at her table. I remember her German kuchen (coffee cake). She made lots of kuchen and it was available to anyone at all times of the day. She made her bread and kuchen from the same warm yeast bread dough. The kuchen was made in large flat pans and was topped with a layer of maple syrup syphoned from the large maple tree in our orchard. She then topped it with crushed black walnuts picked and stored each year from two enormous black walnut trees from the same orchard. I shall never forget how good it tasted any tine of the day and I never tired of that taste.

Every fall in October or November, we joined with our neighbors for a "butchering bee". The men and women would spend all of one day at each farm butchering the winter's supply of meat. The men usually butchered one large beef animal and three or four heavy hogs. Most of the beef was canned in fruit jars by the women. To this day, canned beef and a few homemade noodles is among my fondest of foods! The pork was sliced or chunked in various sized portions and put into twenty or thirty gallon crocks with home rendered lard that was as white as snow. Either the beef or the pork could be made into a fantastic meal in just a few minutes. Maybe I get carried away with my desire for canned beef or salted down pork, but for me there is no better solid food. Wow, what a feed anytime!

Mother raised a lot of chickens, so we had lots of fried chicken throughout the summer and fall. We also had plenty of eggs to eat and sell. We usually milked twelve to fifteen cows. Milking was everybody's job. We had plenty of milk and cream for our home. We churned our own butter. It seems that about the only things we bought were flour, sugar, coffee and tea and a few incidentals. Every Saturday night we would take the excess cream and eggs to town to sell at the creamery. The proceeds would usually take care of the grocery bill. Sometimes there was a little excess money and Mother and Dad would divide it between us four kids. We usually headed for the ice cream and candy store.

Mother was the stabilizing force of our family. During adverse conditions, sickness, severe storms, financial crisis, accidents and other negatives, she could always find something to say or do to eliminate the uncertainty of any negative atmosphere.

I adored my Mother.

Mother - Mary Vogler Jennings - 1942

Chapter 2

Remembering Dad

My dad, Charlie, was an athletic type man of about 180 pounds. He thrived on heavy physical work. He had a great personality and was highly respected. His laugh was contagious. He possessed a shrill whistle and for many years he was among the top contestants in the famous Iowa hog-calling contests.

Dad lived in the day of the horse. Horses were the only means of transportation and farming. There were no tractors available that any of the farmers in our area could afford. Besides, horses were doing a good job. We had several teams of matched horses that were well conditioned and broke to perfection. Most of our horses were sorrel or red roan Belgians. We did have a couple of teams of stocking footed Percherons.

Horse trading was a separate business in Iowa in horse days of buying, selling or trading horses. The horse traders were men who came by the farms trailing their horses with lead ropes tied to the side and end of their wagon. They would come by our farm at thirty to sixty day intervals and Dad would try to trade or sell any horses that we had no further use for because of numerous reasons.

Any horse with a bad disposition was not allowed to

Dad - Charles Jennings

Clayton and Ted Jennings - About 1916

stay on our farm. They were either sold or traded to a horse trader. Any horse or teams of horses that frightened easily were traded without further use. A horse that runs away once can't ever be cured - he will run away again at the first opportunity. The damages of a runaway to human life and property was too great to risk. Occasionally there was a fatality in our community and it was a grievous time. Broken bones, severe cuts and gashes came more often but time healed most of them. Some horses were kickers and would start kicking for no justified reason, sometimes with one hind leg and sometimes with both hind legs - simultaneously. I am sure there were less fatalities in that day of the horse than today

Clayton Jennings - 1918

with the car, pickup, tractor, snowmobile, airplane and three and four wheelers.

Dad taught Ted and I how to handle and drive horses at a very early age, probably eight and ten. We were both so proud when we could handle the horses with but little advise or correction from him. Being able to handle horses was probably our first major accomplishment. He taught us to curry, feed and harness the horses. Our first attempt to harness the horses was an episode to behold, as we had to stand on a short hog trough to get the heavy harnesses up on the backs of the big, gentle horses. This was another accomplishment that made us feel good!

Early one morning Dad told Ted and I to go hitch a team to the sled and bring them to the house where we were to pick up him and Mom. We were going some distance and returning the same day. Ted and I had just passed the test of harnessing, hitching and driving a team. We always listened to Dad closely. Ted and I asked, "Dad, which team do you want us to hitch?" Dad said "We are going a good distance and we want to get back, so hitch the best horses." We asked if he meant Pat and Mike and he said, "Why, of course." And that we did.

Dad bought his first tractor, a "Waterloo Boy" for $700.00. It was the pro and con talk of our area. It took nearly fifty years for the transition from horses to tractors and cars. Now, the harness and horse drawn vehicles are antiques. About the only things left from the draft horse era are scoop shovels, pitchforks, spades, sand shovels and crowbars!

My dad spent every minute of his time that was feasible with my brother Ted and me. He showed and taught us the ins and outs of buying, selling and trading cattle and hogs. We traveled with him by horse and buggy, team and wagon or team and sled. We would cover an area of about 20 miles in diameter. Dad would always hitch our best, strongest, well-mannered horses. They could trot at a fast pace for a couple miles without drawing a long breath. We could cover our township, stopping at most of the farms and dealing on their cattle or hogs in a matter of five or six days a month. We were always invited in where ever we happened to be at meal time. The farmers always seemed happy to feed us.

On Saturdays, holidays and during the summer time we would start out before daylight and get back home long after dark - tired but fulfilled. On these trips Dad would advise us on what to do and what not to do in life if we wanted to be somebody. This was constant advice on all of our trips and at home around the feedlot and barn. We watched and listened to Dad's technique of dealing. It seemed that all his customers liked him. The deals that he made always seemed to be pleasant. He had repeat deals with his customers year after year.

When we were with our dad we watched every move he made. During grain harvest in the summer he usually hauled oats or wheat from the threshing machine to the grain bins. He used a four or five box wagon that held about 100 bushels. Many times we watched him scoop a full load of grain into the bin without a stop or change of pace. He handled the large sized scoop so gracefully with rhythm like a violin player. He would sweat and his entire shirt and cap would be saturated with perspiration. Not until he had finished cleaning the wagon box did he pull out his big red bandana handkerchief (all of two feet square) and wipe his face and neck. He would say, "Boys, sweat and hard work will not hurt you. It will build your muscles and your character!" He would then flex his muscles and he reminded us of a Greek God! I watched my dad flex his muscles nearly every day. I can still visualize it today. We had a full length mirror on one of the walls of our home and he stood in front of it flexing his muscles. It was a ritual with him. So I started flexing my muscles at a really young age - my biceps, my shoulder muscles, and sometimes my stomach muscles in front of my dad's mirror. It seemed that I could see my muscles growing every day and it made me like myself better. I have always had a full length mirror in every house I've lived in. Now at 81 years of age, when I flex my muscles in front of my full length mirror all I see are wrinkles!

Dad could handle a pitchfork just as gracefully as he could the scoop shovel when loading and unloading grain bundles into the threshing machine, pitching hay and cleaning manure out of the barn and cattle shed.

We had every size of scoop and pitchfork known to man and Dad would show us what size to use on the different jobs. Dad always seemed to make hard work a lot of fun. When cleaning out the sheds in the feedlot we always had a manure throwing contest. We would step off a distance of 15 or 20 feet. We would all three line up abreast and take turns throwing a fork full of manure against the wall. Ted and I could reach the wall sometimes and sometimes not. If we hit the wall the manure generally all fell down to the ground. Dad could make the manure stick firmly and high up on the wall. Dad would say "Anyone can sling manure against the wall, but it takes a good man to make it stick!" He was always challenging us for more and better.

My childhood ended abruptly when I was about ten years old. Dad's health failed and he was bedridden for two years. With Dad's counsel, Ted and I stepped into the business as partners. When I was eleven and Ted was thirteen we purchased a shipment of livestock worth $12,000.00 in Humboldt County, Iowa. Ted offered the farmer a check for that amount. Before the farmer's banker would accept the check he called the Livermore, Iowa, bank to see if the check written by "the kid" was good! The Livermore banker said "Did he sign it?" The Humboldt banker replied, "Yes." The Livermore banker said, "Then it's as good as gold."

Ted and I lived and breathed our Dad. We developed a deep desire to become exactly like him. Can you blame us?

I admired my Dad!

Charles and Mary Jenning - 1942

Chapter 3

Dad's Ten Commandments for Ted and Me

1. Boys, be sure to remember your Maker when day is done. You may need him tomorrow.

2. Boys, be gentlemen at all times - it costs you nothing and pays you well.

3. Boys, anger can be your worst enemy - it can ruin or destroy your life. Use disappointment to calm your anger.

4. Boys, don't ever quit - don't ever give up - finish whatever you start as well as you can.

5. Boys, be pleasant at all times - it doesn't cost - it pays big. Pleasantness is admired by all.

6. Boys, don't ever make fun of or laugh at the underprivileged, unfortunate or down-trodden people, but for the grace of your Maker, you could be one of them.

7. Boys, be honest and fair in your talk and dealings - have faith and trust in people.

8. Boys, always keep your word good - let no one defy your word of honor without a fight.

9. Boys, all big business started from zero and progressed with repeat business from satisfied customers.

10. Boys, don't ever get too big for your britches. Don't ever ever take on more or bigger deals than you can keep up with. I've seen it wreck a lot of people.

Chapter 4

Partnership

A partnership is no more and no less than the integrity of the people involved.

The Jennings Brothers, Ted and Clayton Jennings, were involved in the livestock business as partners at a very early age. Ted was twelve and I was ten when our dad became bed-ridden for two years with rheumatoid arthritis. We took over his cattle and hog buying business. We would go to his bed every day and counsel with him and every day he counseled us just right. The continuation of our partnership for nearly forty years must be one of the most unique of partnerships of the land and livestock business. Our partnership was established in about 1925 and continued until 1962, when we divided our partnership. Never once during the tenure of this partnership was there one sharp word of protest or misunderstanding. All during this time of our partnership we had a philosophy of "live and let live" for ourselves and our customers.

Ted and I both raised our families and conducted all our business from one checking account at the First National Bank, Miller, South Dakota. Whatever either of us decided to spend, for business or for pleasure, was checked out of that account. We did not realize that this was an abnormal way of handling a checking account.

From the very beginning of our partnership we flourished. It just seemed that Ted and I saw things much alike and we complemented each other. During the four years (1941/45) that I was in the Navy Ted took care of everything and went right on with the partnership.

As we developed the Hyland Angus Ranch at Highmore, South Dakota, we were fortunate in riding the land and livestock market up from the very low drought years of the 1930's.

Our profits soared which put us in a high income bracket, but we found a remedy for that. We found that the repairs and paint to the numerous sets of buildings and corrals and the many miles of

Clayton, Ted and Margaret Jennings - 1926

fences on the ranches were expenses that the Internal Revenue allowed us to charge off. We could charge off every penny of this upkeep.

We had one or two crews every summer who kept all the buildings and corrals painted and repaired and kept the fences repaired. That's all they did all summer. Lots of people wondered how we could afford to keep these crews working all summer, but the fact was we couldn't afford not to do this as it added much value to every ranch we owned. We took great pride in having our ranches picture perfect and yet practical. Our theme was that all buildings be kept painted white with green trim and green asphalt shingled roofs. All the corrals were painted white with black posts.

During our partnership Ted always lived in Miller, South Dakota. He spent most of his time speculating on cattle and always using the Jennings Brothers bank account. I lived on the Hyland Angus Ranch running the ranch end of our business and speculating on cattle, always using the Jennings Brothers bank account. We never complimented or criticized each other on any gains or losses in the partnership. We expected the best from each other whether we won or lost. Money never was our biggest goal, but achievement was always foremost of our desires.

The success of our partnership was repeat business and our great number of good friends. If you can develop a satisfied customer he will come to you because he likes doing business with you. New customers are hard to find and even harder to sell. People enjoy doing business with people they like.

After dividing our partnership neither one of us has done as well. Our individual achievements have been considerably less. We both have had sporadic ups and downs, up to and including today.

I feel that our partnership would be very difficult to equal. We were able to maintain a life of beauty and success for nearly 40 years of our partnership. We accumulated many good friends along the way.

Chapter 5

Baseball - 1920

When we lived on the farm in Boone County, Iowa, baseball was the big sport of the day. Some of the townships in our rural area organized a baseball team that would play every Sunday and most holidays during the summer. The games were really competitive and it would make you think that every game was as important as the World Series of Baseball.

Clayton and Ted in front of their farm home - about 1916. Man not identified.

The competition was intense and everyone had the desire to win. Everyone - men, women and children - enjoyed the games. The families traveled to a different farm each week to play. Some traveled as far as ten or twelve miles, some by team and buggy and some by team and wagon. When the games were over it was friendship and enjoyment, and the women served lemonade, cake and homemade ice cream.

Most of the farmers in our area had a small pasture of forty to sixty acres where they grazed their milk cows and horses in the summertime. These pastures were turned into baseball diamonds every Sunday. I remember vividly that we left the milk cows in the barn on Sunday morning so the pasture could be made ready for the game. As soon as the ball players arrived, we all went to the pasture to stake out the diamond and mark the baselines with chalk. But first we had to remove all the cow manure from the infield and from a few feet outside the baselines. We had a manure wagon and everyone brought a scoop to load the wagon. The load was hauled far out past the outfield and roughly scattered over the pasture. We did not remove the cow manure in the outfield. The outfielders would slip and slide and were on their own when chasing a fly ball. There was no homerun wall, so anything hit over an outfielder's head was nearly always a homerun. We usually had three umpires, one each for homeplate, leftfield and rightfield. The umpires were picked from the men attending the games.

My dad always played shortstop. He was rated as one of the best. It seems that every man on the team brought his own special bat. I can remember the day Dad gave me his old bat. It was a dull orange color and was full of pock marks but still sound. I cherished that old bat and I had it until after I moved to the Hyland Angus Ranch in 1949. At the ranch we would bat small rocks and it developed many more pock marks.

The bat has since disappeared, except from memory.

Chapter 6

The Day of the Horse

In 1923 when I was almost ten years old and still living in Boone, Iowa, I had one of the greatest "growing up" experiences of my life.

Raymond Vogler, my mother's brother, lived on a farm a few miles north of Boone. He came to town one day to get me to do some work with him that would last about two or three weeks. Uncle Raymond did considerable farming and raised Belgian draft horses.

He took me out to the barnyard and showed me a whole yard full of big red roan and sorrel Belgian mares. He said we were going to start breeding these mares the next morning and he would show and tell me what I needed to do.

We went to another barn and saw a couple of three year old red roan Belgian stallions that he used to breed the mares. We then went out to the circular patio adjoining the barns. It was about one hundred feet in diameter. He walked around the circle with me and said, "Clayton, you will lead one mare at a time from the barn. You will walk in a circle around the pen leading the mare at either a walk or a trot, whichever the mare wishes to do."

He told me he would lead one of the stallions about thirty to forty feet behind me and the mare. He would motion to me when the time was right and I would lead the mare directly to the snorting pole and tie her securely to the pole. I would quickly get on the other side and away from any danger. Then he would take over.

My uncle was rated an expert in breeding draft horses, so I had full confidence in him and the handling of the horses.

Early the next morning we went out to the barn and stalled the mares. We fed each mare and each stallion a bucket of oats and some fresh hay. We came back to the house and had a hearty breakfast. After breakfast we went out to try the mares. Uncle Raymond had explained to me thoroughly the procedure we were going to use. I understood it well. It was simple but very important. These were big draft horses weighing up toward a ton each and I was a ten year old boy hoping I could do a man's job. I wasn't exactly scared but I had an awesome feeling - the horses were huge and I felt so small.

I led my first mare out of the barn. She was very gentle. We went to the patio and started our circular walk. Then came Uncle Raymond leading one of the stallions. He was about forty feet behind me. Within a few seconds the air was filled with horse mating sounds. It was evident both horses knew what was to be. My mare whinnied loud and clear then changed to a soft whinny. It was constant and she was prancing all the while.

The stud would prance and highstep and sidestep. He would snort as loud as any animal I had heard. He would blow out his nostrils and it looked like a trumpet horn. This went on for several minutes. The stallion was ready.

My uncle pointed toward the snorting pole. I broke the circle and took the mare directly to the snorting pole. I slid under it and brought the rope on around, wrapped it several times and tied it as securely as I could. Then I took my distance out of danger.

My uncle would bring the stallion up to the mare. If she was ready, the breeding process continued until completed. Then I took the mare back to her stall and my uncle returned the stallion to his stall, but if the mare was not ready or willing she would squeal and viciously kick at him with both hind feet. Uncle Raymond would lead the stallion away and I would take the mare back to her stall. We would try her again the next day. Uncle Raymond's two young studs could breed six to eight mares a day.

In a little over two weeks we had bred all of Uncle Raymond's mares plus about a dozen more that belonged to the neighbors, who brought the mares over when they were in heat. This was good business for my uncle as the service fees on the top stallions that he had were very lucrative. This was the day of the horse. They were everything in farming and transportation.

One day when there was not much going on with the mares, my uncle said, "Let's get in my car and go over to Grant Good's farm." He wanted to show me Farceur, the greatest Belgian stallion the world had ever known. That idea thrilled me. I had never met Grant Good but I had heard many times about him being the premier breeder of draft horses. We drove to Ogden, Iowa, which was about

Grant Good farm near Odgen, Iowa. Before Farceur's barn was built. About 1915

twelve or fifteen miles and then a mile and half northeast of Ogden to Oakdale Farms owned by Grant Good. As we came toward the farm we could see a big beautiful set of white buildings. We spotted Grant standing right in front of a large barn he had built for his mares. The barn was rated as the largest hip roof barn in Iowa. It was 120 feet long with very large hay storage and all boxstalls for the horses below. It was a masterpiece of a draft horse barn.

Grant seemed pleased to see us both and wanted to show us the rest of the buildings. He was a gentleman deluxe kind of fellow and his soft voice would pierce and influence everyone. He had an air of unique individualism that stuck with me.

We walked from the large barn over the entire farmstead. The several other barns and granaries were all well kept - then came the climax. Just across the driveway from his beautiful home was a small hip-roof barn. We went through a small gate to a door. Grant said, "Step aside and I'll let Farceur out to exercise." Out of the door into the exercise pen of an acre or two came a beautiful red roan Belgian stallion. He came out in grand style, prancing with his head high in the air and tail flashing behind him. He made everyone know he was the Grand Champion of the horse kingdom. We went into the barn that Grant had designed especially for Farceur. His padded stall was one half of the barn. The other half was oats and hay storage with an overhead loft for hay and straw. After showing us everything he invited us to the house so he could tell us the whole Farceur story.

We sat around the kitchen table having coffee and cookies and Grant told us the following story that has been lasting to me.

Grant said he became interested in Belgian horses at an early age. He started showing horses at fairs and exhibitions. In 1911 he started importing good horses from Belgium and France making sixteen trips across the ocean. In 1917 at Cedar Falls, Iowa, William Crownover had a draft horse dispersal sale. That's where Grant purchased Farceur, the only World's Grand Champion Belgian Stallion known. Crownover had shown Farceur all over Europe before he imported him to the United States. He was undefeated in Europe. Farceur was then shown in the United States and Canada and it was then that he was awarded the World's Grand Champion Belgian Stallion Banner. Grant Good paid $47,500.00 for him.

Grant told us that this was a lot of money, but he believed in the horse so much that before the sale he went around and talked with

Grant Good and the World's Grand Champion Belgian Stallion, Farceur, which was purchased in 1917 for a record price of $47,500.00.

his neighbors. They all wanted a colt out of Farceur and they would pay Grant in advance a stud fee of $500 to $1000 for his guarantee of a standing suckling colt. With this show of support from his neighbors, Grant was able to buy this champion draft horse. I was amazed at the detail with which he told us of this draft horse deal.

After purchasing Farceur, Grant started setting records with his Belgians. He was the longest running exhibitor and one of the largest importers of Belgians. He was the only person to use four modes of transportation - truck, ship, rail, and air.

Though Farceur was unbeatable as a show horse his greatest fame was as a sire. The wonderful similiarity of the colts from all types of mares marked him as the most prepotent sire of his day.

About six months after I saw Farceur, he died mysteriously on Christmas Eve 1923 while the Good family was enjoying their dinner just a short distance from his barn. He was still alive when they discovered what had happened. They called the veterinarian from Boone but he was unable to save him. Grant had this big stallion buried in his stall in the barn especially built for him. This was a sad day for the Good family and whole horse world.

My family kept in close contact with Grant Good and his family as my Uncle Raymond married Grant's daughter Mabel. We would visit the Good farm at least once a year.

In later years Grant also owned the worlds's largest Belgian horse. He was foaled in 1928 and named Brooklyn Supreme. He was shown in a circus sideshow by Ralph Fogelman for several years. He was given to Grant Good as payment for a "loan" of a Good stallion to be used on five mares owned by another breeder, but raised by Grant Good. Brooklyn Supreme attained his greatest weight in 1939 when shown at the San Francisco World's Fair - 3180 pounds - recognized as the world's largest horse in the Guinness Book of World Records.

Grant Good was active in community and state affairs. He was justice of the peace in Boone County, Iowa. He served two terms in the early 1930's and again three terms from 1947 to 1953 in the Iowa State Legislature.

Grant Good was one of the biggest gamblers of all time in the horse business. Every step of his involvement with Belgian horses created great risks - shipping long distances including overseas - injuries which male animals can receive in the breeding process can end their usefulness - exposure to diseases both foreign and

Brooklyn Supreme - world's largest horse - owned by Grant Good, Ogden, Iowa

domestic. These were part of the gambles he was willing to take to gain the success that was always in sight as his reward. Farceur, by far, was his biggest gamble, but the best buy he ever made.

Considering today's money it would be prohibitive to own a horse like Farceur but that was the day of the horse.

Chapter 7

Ristau's Pool Hall

My dad moved our family from Boone, Iowa, to Livermore, Iowa, in 1924. Livermore was a little northwest Iowa town of barely 500 people. It's only claim to notoriety was during the prohibition days when the bootleggers and rum runners congregated there. Many people in the area made their own homebrew, the best to be found anywhere. Famous big bands played for dances in Livermore, which brought many people to town to dance at the large dance hall. Livermore developed a reputation all over the state and was referred to as "Liquormore".

I was eleven years old when we moved to Livermore. It seemed that the boys my age didn't have any extra-curricular activities, except the pool hall, and high school sports of basketball, football, baseball and track. The pool hall was an ancient two-story building right in the center of main street, which was one city block.

Hank Ristau, a farmer from north of Livermore, owned the pool hall, which he personally took care of himself. He kept it open from 5 p.m. until 12 midnight. He had four pool tables and one billiard table and most of the time every table was full with two, four or more players for each game at five cents a pool cue per game.

Hank was a big husky man weighing no less than 240 pounds. He had a gruff voice that would scare you when you talked to him, but after the first meeting you learned to like him. He had a heart as big as the whole outdoors. He would let anyone play pool anytime, especially the kids, even if they didn't have any money. To pay their bill, he would have them do jobs around the pool hall or on his farm. Some of these kids became real pool sharks. It was a real source of entertainment for all of us.

There was very little money in those days so people traded something for something else. In this case, the boys traded labor for credit at the pool hall.

Hank usually burned coal to heat the pool hall. In 1929 or 1930 when the economy collapsed on all

Clayton and Ted Jennings about 1927.
Woman not identified.

commodities the farmers had to sell their ear corn for ten cents per bushel. When Hank tried to sell his ear corn (and he had a lot of it), the best bid he could get was eight cents per bushel - delivered. Hank bowed his neck and said to hell with that. "I'll burn my own corn in my own pool hall!" And he did!

Hank told all the boys who didn't have any money to stop by the pool hall when the ear corn was hauled from his farm to the pool hall and they could shovel it into the basement and bins. Hank gave the boys something to do and besides the corn burned well and made real good heat.

The pool hall was nearly always full during the open hours. It was the best and only source of recreation for high school age kids. Only occasionally would there be two or three girls come into the pool hall. They didn't stay long as we boys would make fun of them, ridicule, and tease them.

Most of the guys in my group who hung together were freshman and sophomores in high school, but we had one senior boy that hung out with our crowd. His name was Cassady. He was tall and more mature than the rest of the group. He was very handsome and had a smooth tongue. Everyone liked him. In fact, he was kind of our leader. It seems that with every game of pool that we played we talked about the girls and Cassady just listened. One day Cassady broke into our conversation loud and clear and said, "If you guys really want to know how to treat the girls, I can tell you, but you have got to listen." He told us that we had been entirely wrong when talking to the girls and he gave us a list of things we must do. He said that we must quit ridiculing them and making fun of them and start being pleasant because all girls like a pleasant guy and none like a miserable guy. "Boys, you have been treating the girls exactly opposite of the way they would like to be treated. You must be gentle, considerate and pleasant. Boys, all the girls like a gentleman and like to be treated like a lady."

Cassady always called us "boys". He told us that we all had been a bunch of smart aleck bums with the girls. He told us we would have to completely change our style and tactics.

I was one of these smart aleck bums and his advice to us soaked in. I think at this time we changed for the better. We became pleasant and showed respect for others. The girls started liking us.

This advice that Cassady gave us has helped me all through life. In this world I have found that you must give something to get something!

Chapter 8

Threshing and Homebrew

When I was about twelve years old and living in Livermore, Iowa, I was asked by a local farmer, Matt Kohlhaas, to be one of his bundle haulers on his threshing crew. He came to our home early one morning in August as one of his haulers had been injured and he needed me to keep a full crew running.

Matt knew I could handle a team of horses and I could fill in for the injured man as it was highly important to keep a full crew.

He took me out to his farm and showed me the team of horses, a matched pair - black with white stocking feet - and the bundle rack I was to use. I felt sure I could handle the horses in the field where I would pitch the bundles of oats on the bundle rack, but I had some doubts about driving the team up to the feeder of the threshing machine. The threshing machine was powered by a very noisy steam engine and I was afraid it would keep the horses on edge. On nearly every threshing crew there was at least one runaway every fall because of the noisy steam engines. It was always a real mess.

Matt encouraged me and said he knew I could get some help if I needed it when pulling up to the feeder of the threshing machine.

He gave me a good three tined pitchfork and showed me the field of oats that we would be hauling from to the threshing machine. I liked my team better every day. They stopped and started at my command and never showed signs of spookiness.

Everything went along as I had hoped the first morning and at noon everyone unhitched their teams of horses and lead them over to the water tank in the farmyard for a drink. Then we tied them to the side of the bundle racks and we all headed to the farmer's house for dinner.

The weather was hot and humid and as we entered the farmyard I could see under a large shade tree a big container filled with ice and homebrew. This was almost a 100% German ancestry community and they loved their homebrew. The bottles were large, nearly a quart each and everyone took a bottle. One of the fellows took the cap off one and handed it to me. I took the bottle and watched all the other fellows tipping their bottle up and taking a drink and they expected me to do the same. I tipped my bottle up about as often as the men did, but I held it to a small sip each time. But it still took its toll on me.

This was the first alcohol of any kind I had ever tasted. Everyone was laughing and making jokes about the homebrew. I knew they expected me to be a man.

It tasted pretty good, but soon I got dizzy and I had the feeling I was trying to hang onto the turning world. I never felt so helpless in my life. I knew I had to do something. I noticed the outhouse out back, so I kinda staggered and wobbled out there. The outhouse seemed to be going round and round. I poured most of the bottle of homebrew into the hole in the outhouse and went back to the men. I ate a good big dinner and that helped with the dizziness and sick feeling and I was able to continue my job hauling bundles.

I got by with that first bottle so I used the same routine every day through the threshing period of a couple weeks.

With this little finesse with the homebrew I finished my job as a bundle hauler. Matt paid me well and this was one of the unforgettable experiences of my life.

Chapter 9

Watermelon Mania

My group in Livermore had a mania for stealing watermelons. Many of the farmers in the area raised watermelons for their own use and some on a commercial basis. Usually the melon patches were on either side of the railroad tracks near Livermore and down to the Des Moines River about two miles away.

We usually did our thievery on moonlit nights so we could find the biggest melons. We would walk down the railroad track making a game of seeing who could walk the farthest on the rail without falling off. If a slow moving freight happened to be going our way we would hop in an open door of an empty boxcar and ride to the patch. We would jump off when the train passed the patch that we wanted to raid that night.

Every fall we would spot the patches that we thought had the biggest ripe melons. We would hurry through the patch searching for the largest melons and plug them with a V-shaped incision into the heart with a jack-knife. If they were ripe we would steal them. If they were green we would leave them in the patch. The plugged melons would not ripen but would rot and were of no use to the farmer.

We would take the biggest ripe melons we could find back to the railroad tracks. The melons were big and heavy and one was all each of us could carry. We sat on the tracks and broke the melons open by hitting them on the rails. We would take our jack-knives and cut out the heart and eat it. Any melons that we took were more than we could eat so we just left what we didn't want on the railroad tracks.

We thought this was great sport, but all of us learned our lesson in one unforgettable night of watermelon stealing!

We seldom ever went to the same patch two nights in a row. We had heard that sometimes the farmers would be waiting at the edge of their patch with a 12 gauge shotgun and fire buckshot at any thieves in his patch. The buckshot wasn't deadly but would scatter and sting if it hit you.

This one patch had particularly large sweet melons. We decided to raid it again. The owner of the patch was a real decent man and there was no question that he would have given us all the melons we could eat if we would have asked. But we flourished on our sneakiness, selfishness, greediness and the idea that we were real clever kids.

So back to the same patch we went, going through the same routine of finding the largest melon, plugging it and if it was ripe we took it. If it was green we left it to

Clayton and Ted Jennings about 1928

rot on the vine. We carried them back to the railroad tracks. We sat on the tracks eating all we could. We were unaware of what was about to happen to us.

We didn't know it at the time but the farmer was ready for us. He had a solution and purpose that would cure all our real ills. He took a ten cc syringe with a very long needle and filled it with a liquid laxative. He went to his patch and selected the largest ripe melons in the part of the patch he thought might be raided. He inserted the long needle into the heart of the melons (which we always ate) and injected it with one cc of the laxative. Then he went back to his house to wait for the results.

The word spread quickly around Livermore the next day about the boys who were unable to go to school because of a severe case of diarrhea. This was the most severe laxative I had ever had in my lifetime. Everyone knew who the watermelon thieves were. We became known as the "Shitty Thieves"!

Speaking for myself and the other boys, I'm sure these were the last melons any of us ever stole in our lives. We had learned our lesson!

The memory of my many fast trips to the outhouse in our backyard is still vivid in my mind!

Chapter 10

Ted Jennings - 440 Yards

As you read this chapter you may think I'm one of the biggest braggarts in the business, but be what it may it is one of my most lasting inspirations of my life and among my greatest feelings of joy.

My brother Ted was a pretty good athlete during his four years of high school in the little town of Livermore, population of barely 500. He was always on the first team in football, basketball and track. He was just average in football and basketball, but he was superior in track, especially in the 440 yard dash.

As a freshman and sophomore he won most of the 440 yard dash events. But was beaten occasionally but by a small margin. As a junior and senior he won every 440 yard dash event that I am aware of because of some real cute coaching by O. J. Cayou. Coach Cayou said to him, "Ted, it matters not who wins the first 100 yards in the 440 yard dash, but who wins the LAST 100 yards!" Ted always trained with that in mind.

I can still visualize Ted in a race. He was usually the smallest fellow in the race. He probably didn't weigh over 130 pounds at his peak, but he had a pair of legs second to none and the stamina of a horse.

Each year the opposing teams were out to beat Ted Jennings, but they never did beat him. He was cunning in his approach to each race. If the racers were facing the wind and that happened occasionally, he would intentionally aim to be the last in the pack the first 100 or 200 yards, letting the other runners break the wind and saving his energy, but when he thought the time was right he would turn on the steam and drive by the whole pack and win the race - maybe by 40 or 50 yards. After one race that Ted had won, the biggest boy in the race, who came in second, and who Ted had followed behind most of the race said to Ted, "Where the hell did you come from?" One of the other racers said, "I didn't see him either until the last 100 yards!"

I was always on the sidelines screaming and yelling at him to "get going" while he was in the middle and sometimes in the last of the pack. I'm sure he couldn't hear me but he always turned on the steam and ran right by all the runners. He was a true sensation and everyone admired his courage, determination and unlimited wind.

Each time that he won by big margins I'd say, "Boys, I told you he'd do it, didn't I?"

The one regret I have is that the little town of Livermore could not afford to take a "one-man" track team to the Iowa State Track Meet at the Drake Field House in Des Moines - because I personally think he could have won the state 440 yard dash in a cakewalk.

Ted Jennings ran his life just the way he ran the 440 yard dash - with courage, determination and unlimited wind!

Ted Jennings - 1930

PART II
1932 - 1946

I graduated from Livermore, Iowa, high school in 1932 and immediately went to eastern South Dakota to buy pigs. South Dakota was in the midst of the worst drought the state had ever experienced and pigs were cheap and plentiful.

In 1934 I traveled farther west around Pierre, South Dakota, and started to buy cattle and ship them to Iowa for Ted to merchandise. There were many cattle for sale as the drought was continuing.

In spite of the drought, I liked South Dakota and decided to stay. My first home was the Brown Hotel in Miller. I continued to buy cattle in South Dakota and surrounding states and ship them to Ted in Iowa. We had a very lucrative business.

Following the drought, livestock auction barns began to spring up in this part of the country. In 1939 Jim Magness and I started the auction barn in Miller.

On December 7th, 1941, the Japanese bombed Pearl Harbor. I felt it my duty to enlist in the Navy, so Ted moved his family to South Dakota to manage the salebarn with Jim Magness.

When I returned from the Navy in 1945, Ted and I decided to sell the salebarn and develop the Hyland Angus Ranch.

Chapter 11

Ed Hartland

During the middle and late 1930's I established a lot of cattle business for the Jennings Brothers in the area west and north of Ft. Pierre, South Dakota. During certain seasons of the year I would ship one or two trainloads of cattle to the cornbelt each week. We had one very good customer, Louis Dinklage of Wisner, Nebraska, who bought several trainloads of cattle from me mostly in the months of August, September and October. Louis owned a large feedlot and liked to feed big two and three year old steers weighing from 1000 to 1200 pounds.

I had started to deal with the area ranchers and encouraged them to sell their cattle to me on a dollars per head basis delivered to the railroad nearest to their ranch. We did a lot of visiting about it and my end of the story for them was that they could depend on "so many total dollars for so many cattle" when they got to the railroad stockyards. They had no gamble with weighing them and using the weight and price per pound basis. They were happy with the dollars per head price as they could plan their business somewhat ahead. Occasionally the railroad scales would not be working properly and that would make a bigger gamble for both of us.

I, in particular, liked to do business on the dollars per head basis as I could guess and gamble with the ranchers and they liked it also.

This buying of nearly everyone's cattle by the head was a precedent that I developed during the 1930's and have continued all through my life. During the 1930's and until I went to the Navy in 1942, practically all of the cattle I bought was on the dollars per head basis.

Some of the area ranchers that I did business with every year were: Martin Samuelson, Milt Elkins, Hedman Brothers, Roy Norman, Alex Stoesser, Roseth Ranch, Ansgar Hoagie, Dr. Knox, Fischer Brothers, Bill Krueger and Rhodes Brothers. All of the ranchers had strictly top quality Hereford-bred cattle. The blacks had not invaded this Hereford country yet.

I always had railroad cars ordered a week in advance of the date of the shipment. I had fifty-five railroad cars in Ft. Pierre for the shipment the last week in October. I had most of the steers bought and every one of them by the per head basis. Many times several of the ranchers would drive their cattle together bringing large numbers at a time to the railroad stockyards. We would sort them for brand and pay number for each rancher. I had bought all of these cattle on the per head basis.

I had one more ranch to go yet to finish the trainload shipment of cattle that was destined for the Dinklage Yards in Wisner, Nebraska. It was Ed Hartland who had a good big ranch south of Ft. Pierre. He had four or five hundred big two year old steers to sell. They were weighing from 1000 to 1250 lbs. I liked his cattle really well. I had bought them the previous two or three years on the dollars per head basis and he always seemed satisfied. I told him that if I bought them I would need to have them at the Ft. Pierre railroad stockyards Friday or Saturday. I would let him know. I asked him how many dollars per head he wanted for 400 of his heaviest steers.

Ed said, "Clayton, I want to sell these steers by the pound." He said it quite firmly. It really surprised me and I said "Ed, I bought the rest of the trainload of steers by the head. You always sold yours to me by the head the past few years and you always seemed satisfied with the deal." I told him I would like to finish this trainload of steers on the dollars per head basis. I told him I thought I could give him more than by weighing them. I tried every way to convince him that he would be more satisfied with the price per head basis when he got them to town.

The more I talked the more convincing he was that he wanted to sell by the pound. He said that he had two bobtail 14' trucks as did several of his neighbors and they agreed to help him haul them to Ft. Pierre. I asked him what kind of weighing conditions would I have if he hauled them in.

Ed went into elaborate detail of how he would handle the weighing condition on the steers. He said he would gather all the steers the afternoon before he delivered them to the railroad yards in Ft. Pierre. He would put them in the corrals and cover the water tanks so they would be off water all night. He said I would have excellent weighing conditions when considering the overnight shrink they would have standing in the corrals off feed and water. Then he took me down to the corrals to show me where he would put them for the overnight stand. His corrals were big and adequate. There was no sign of feed in the yards and I felt sure he would take the water away from them as he agreed.

The last thing I said to Ed was that I would let him know what day I needed them, Friday or Saturday. He agreed to start hauling at daylight to the Ft. Pierre railroad yards. We would start weighing them as soon as the last steer was unloaded. That was the deal we made. Ed stuck out his big hand and shook mine firmly, and that was the handshake.

I was satisfied with this manner of handling them but I wanted the full trainload bought on a per head basis, so I was somewhat disappointed.

At the time I felt everything was well and good with the deal, but I had a funny feeling about his strong insistence for selling the steers by the pound instead of by the head.

Tommy Johnson from Livermore, Iowa, was working for me. He was riding with me and heard the whole deal. As we pulled out of the yard Tommy surmised the same as I did. Why was he so insistent - but that was his right.

The evening before Ed Hartland was to deliver the steers, Tommy and I were in a bar in Ft. Pierre talking with a lot of ranchers and townspeople and we literally helped close the bar at 1 o'clock. Then we decided to go to the Tumble Inn, an after-hour place where good food was served and people got together.

Tommy and I had talked about this situation ever since I made the deal and we thought - there's something wrong with this deal with Ed Hartland. It was about 2:30 o'clock in the morning when we finished our lunch and business. One of us came up with the idea to drive down to Hartland's Ranch to check the steers in his yards.

It was a moonlight night and when we came to the ranch we turned our lights off and drove to the corrals. I didn't want to believe what I saw! There was green cured hay three feet deep around the inside of each corral. The steers were eating and laying on it. The water tanks were full from the artesian flow. The steers were as full as goats from eating the fresh hay and drinking the water. It would be crucifixion for me to pay on that kind of weights. All this time we were suspicious but couldn't believe this man would do this. We stayed just long enough to check each corral and found the fill on the steers was identical. Then we pulled out and went back to town.

I had to be up by daylight so I didn't get much sleep. I decided I wouldn't say anything until Ed made his next move. I was highly disappointed as this was the first betrayal of me and the handshake in this part of the country.

We were at the yards early and before a hoof of cattle came to the yards, here came Ed Hartland in his vehicle. He jumped out and called me over.

Ed said, "Clayton, I made a deal with you and I didn't keep my word. Why I didn't, God only knows. The cattle got some hay and water and filled up abnormally and I promised you that I would keep them off hay and water for an overnight shrink and I didn't do it. I have never done anything like this in my entire life and I am sick as a dog about it."

Ed continued, "The steers will be coming in and I won't be here. You weigh the cattle and shrink them whatever percent you think is right and I will be satisfied."

I didn't aim to say a word and I didn't. Ed did all the talking, turned around and left in his vehicle.

As Ed's steers were unloaded we observed and weighed them. They weighed really well because of the fill of water and hay. Normally in those days a 3% shrink was adequate, but these steers were super full. I decided the steers should be shrunk 5% to make then equivalent to the rest of the cattle on the trainload. When Jennings Brothers had a customer like Louis Dinklage who bought many trainloads of cattle from us for numerous years we were committed to ourselves to look out for his interest and there was no way I would sell him hay and water. I had time right then to figure the steers and make out his invoice and check. The excess fill on these steers was equivalent to 3/4th of a carload of steers.

Ed came back in the late afternoon, just as we finished loading the railroad cars with the steers. I called Ed off to the side of the scale and showed him the invoice. He told me that they brought more than he thought they might.

I gave Ed his invoice and check. He shook my hand vigorously and said, "Thank you. Please forgive me!" He got into his vehicle and left.

Since that time until Ed's death we were friends. I must rate him as a good man. We all make mistakes, but he corrected his and restored my faith in humanity.

Chapter 12

Knipplings—The Hat Brand Ranch

In the early 1930's when I first came to South Dakota I had the distinct privilege of stopping at the Knippling Brothers "Hat Brand Ranch" of Gann Valley, South Dakota, where Joe and Lambert Knippling operated a cattle and horse operation and they were struggling with anthrax and brucellosis. Their ranch was stocked with Hereford cows, which are still their mainstay today. They showed me around the entire ranch and treated me with real concern. Their time and ranch gave me a great inspiration. I was a farm kid from Iowa until that time and in this day's time I decided I wanted to be in the cattle and ranch business. I have been on the ranch sometime during every year since, except my time in the Navy (1941 to 1945). This has been a model ranch to me and I declare that it is one of the great ranches I have had the privilege to deal with.

The Knippling Brothers Ranch today is a symbol of a thriving livestock enterprise - but this has not always been the case. In their early ranching years their very existence was in danger of being destroyed by two livestock disease menaces - anthrax and brucellosis.

Joe Knippling said, "Anthrax kept us broke from 1912 to 1936." Their losses continued over the years and many remedies were tried, but nothing worked. The anthrax was everywhere and the brucellosis was depressing their calf crop to 60%.

The battle against disease began in 1912 when John Knippling, father of Joe and Lambert, was riding fence and found a dead steer belonging to his neighbor along the fenceline. John pulled it onto

Joe and Lambert Knippling

his property and skinned it. He then dragged the carcass across the range to a washout. Less than a month later, 35 percent of his own cattle were dead as were some of his horses and most of his hogs.

Although no one realized it, anthrax had struck. The carcass of the dead steer infected the ground where it was skinned and the blood infected the range over which it had been dragged.

When new fatalities were disposed of, and because very little was known of the cause of death or of the precautions to take with their remains, more blood was spewn, more carcasses were buried and a new crop of death was seeded into the soil in the form of anthrax spores.

Not until 1936 did the Knipplings get a breakthrough. They contacted the Cutter Laboratories in Berkeley, California, and they suggested a comparatively new anthrax vaccine and a vaccine for the brucellosis. Knipplings followed a rigid herd health program and both vaccines worked.

It can be said that the establishment of sound animal health on this ranch rescued it from economic strangulation and literally opened the gate to success - it spelled the difference between a small, doomed herd in 1936 and a resultant herd which now numbers about 2500 head in cows alone.

Their ranch is practical and feasible for livestock. Never has any of the ranch been overgrazed, except in a few occasions of drought years. The philosophy of their cattle operation is not to over-graze completely to the roots, but graze half the growth of grass, leaving half for the next year which has proven to be a safe and sound policy. This ranch is an ocean of beautiful native grasses that are as potent as any grasses on earth and alfalfa divided into numerous pastures to fit the purpose. There are eighty-five well-fenced pastures, the largest which is six sections (3840 acres) and the smallest thirty acres. There are approximately two hundred and fifty miles of three and four wire outside and cross fences.

The Knipplings have always been willing to spend money for the overall betterment of the ranch even though there are risks involved. During the very severe drought of 1976 they bought an irrigated farm near their ranch to ensure a feed crop for their many cattle. The irrigated fields are a half mile from the Missouri River. As it turned out, 1976 was one of the most severe one-year droughts in this section of South Dakota and it totalled out many of the ranchers in the central part of the state. The Knipplings planted corn on as much of the irrigated land as possible and it gave them a feed supply of real volume and prevented them from having to sell other than the normal amount of cattle. Yes the land, about sixteen hundred acres (530 acres are irrigated), paid for itself in one single year and it proved to be one of the best moves made by the Knippling Brothers in the history of the ranch. Now they feed with con-

Registered Hereford cattle on the Knippling Ranch

Branding and working calves on the Knippling Ranch. l to r: Jerry Knippling, Clayton Knippling, Kenny Wulf, John Abernathy, Bill King and Randy Knippling

fidence knowing that this strip of irrigated land will protect them from forced sales of their cattle. The nature of South Dakota is that there are real risks - and if you are not willing to take the necessary risks you might survive but you will not prosper! The Knipplings were and are of the type willing to take the risks for a better life for themselves and their families. They had been broke for numerous years during the 1920's and 1930's, but that did not stop them. They kept trying new methods in pursuit of a successful operation and that they have today. They have gained a better life for all concerned. I would have to say that they have, as of today, one of the highest financial successes of all the ranches of South Dakota.

The history of South Dakota will tell you that many ranchers have gone completely broke but have then gone on to gain much prestige and wealth in a lifetime. They refused to accept a life of doom and gloom.

The Knippling Ranch today consists of thirty five thousand acres of deeded land and fifteen thousand acres of leased land of gently rolling hills of great beauty with valleys interspersed throughout. Besides the wonderful native grasses and alfalfa on this ranch there is an added asset that is impossible to figure its worth to the ranch. It is Elm Creek, a lazy gentle winding creek that meanders like a snake through the middle of the Knippling Ranch. It is lined with medium sized trees that provide shade and shelter for the livestock. Cattle know this ranch by instinct and when there is a blizzard or rainstorm brewing anytime, they will head to the creek and have the best shelter known to mankind. It affords them better protection than any building ever built. When the storm subsides they go back to the grass on the hillsides. If needed they can drill a shallow well anyplace along Elm Creek for fresh pure water that can never be pumped dry even in dry years. I know Elm Creek well as it ran through the middle of the Hyland Angus South Ranch on its way to Knipplings and then to the Missouri River.

The ranch also has nine flowing artesian wells on the south half that are 775 feet to 1300 feet deep depending on the closeness to the river, with about 12 miles of pipeline running from the wells to tanks in the pastures. They also have 150 stock dams scattered over the ranch.

The Knippling Ranch supports 2200 commercial cows and 300 registered Hereford cows, 1000 carryover bred heifers each year, 400 light steer calves and 130 yearling bulls that they sell at their

Miller Livestock Sales Company, Miller, SD

Jay Anderberg, owner of the Miller Livestock Sales Company and Clayton Jennings

special annual sale every February at the ranch. They have developed an excellent way of merchandising their cattle. They first started selling some of their cattle at the Miller Livestock Auction in the early 1940's. They now sell about 90% of their cattle at the Miller Livestock Auction and with the magnificent efforts of Jay Anderberg, the present owner, they have created a big demand for their cattle with many repeat buyers every year. The Knippling "Hat Brand" cattle have great uniformity of high quality and the demand is always intense. The other 10% are sold by private treaty at the ranch.

The John Knippling family settled in the Gann Valley, South Dakota, area in 1910. Joe and Lambert bought out their father in 1937 and continued to expand with Hereford cattle. Today the ranch is run by Joe's three sons, Don, Jerald and Clayton, as a family corporation which is still very successful today. All share equally in the responsibilities but each has a specific area of interest for which they are individually responsible. Fifth generation Knipplings are now learning the ranching business.

These Knipplings have gained experience on the job. They grew up learning the ranching business. There are no extravaganzas on this ranch, but all their facilities and equipment are modern and up-to-date. Each of the three brothers have a new modern home for top-notch living on the ranch only a few miles apart.

The Knipplings have always been a family that enjoys living and want to let others live. They are always willing to participate and cooperate in community and livestock affairs. Now I would have to rate them as one of the great ranching families of South Dakota.

One day while I was visiting Joe at the ranch he told me the following story:

When Joe was a young man the area was infested with lots of rattlesnakes. Rattlesnakes are very poisonous and medical attention is required immediately after the venom enters a person's body.

Joe told me that early one morning he saddled up one of his strongest and best horses as he was going to spend all day fixing fence. He carried a wire stretcher, wire clippers, some pliers and staples with him. He was to ride the fences and repair any broken wires or gates. He thought he could cover forty or fifty miles of fence on the ranch and get back about dark.

He was getting along fine and had fixed several breaks in the fence as he went along. Then he came upon a double break in the wire fence. He got out the wire stretcher and proceeded to hook it to one of the breaks. As Joe pulled on the stretcher rope, it broke from the tension on it and Joe fell backwards. As he fell he heard the rattle of a rattlesnake, but he had no control of himself and he lit on his back with his feet in the air right on the snake. Joe felt sure the snake had bit him and it was a frightening experience to say the least. He had all kinds of thoughts - it was the most horrible situation that could be - he was on horseback and at least 15 miles from anywhere. He would need a doctor as soon as possible, as time is limited when bitten by a poisonous snake. When Joe finally got on his feet, he observed the snake coiled and still rattling, but it had a good sized gopher half way down its throat - so the snake was unable to strike him. A great feeling of relief came over Joe. He killed the snake with his wire cutters and continued to repair the fence.

1995 Annual Production Sale at the Knippling Ranch; Jerry & Ardyth; Mary Lou and Don; Evelyn and Clayton

Joe had a good feeling, but all the rest of the day whenever he stopped to repair more of the fence he was cautious and searched the prairie for snakes before he got off his horse.

One of the most memorable reminiscences I have of Joe Knippling was during WWII in 1944 when I was serving on the South Sea Island of New Georgia (no man's land). We were in constant combat with the Japanese. Things were tough - the heat - the mosquitoes - the heavy gunfire in the jungle and the bombs coming by air. About all we had to look forward to was mail call.

At mail call one day we received some mail, about 30 days overdue, and among my letters was one from Joe Knippling. He told me they had just had a new son and they named Clayton - after me.

My whole being was revived to hear from such a good friend. It gave me a great feeling to have such an honor bestowed upon me and I shall always cherish that letter.

Donald, Jerald and Clayton Knippling live by the same philosophy their father lived by. "Have a love of livestock. Be alert and adaptable to market trends and to new improved ideas. AND work hard!.

Chapter 13

Duff

My brother-in-law Kenneth "Duff" Howard grew up in the same area of the town of Livermore, Iowa, as I did. In fact we were always very fond of each other. He became one of the bankers in Livermore and we did business with his bank.

Duff was a natural born comedian and actor. We were always trying to belittle each other and we pulled some of the severest of pranks.

I left Iowa for South Dakota as soon as I graduated from high school in 1932. Duff seemed to align his fall vacation so he could

Duff Howard - early 1930's

come to South Dakota and spend as much time with me as possible. He was always interested in what I was doing and everytime we got together it was a fun time. He liked to ride with me when I went out and bought cattle on the ranches in western South Dakota.

His trip every year was based on coming to visit me and I had plenty of pranks lined up to embarrass and humiliate him. I never figured out how I could like him so much and still do such mean things to him. But he loved every minute of it.

One fall during the late 30's we were shipping quite a lot of steers out of western South Dakota to the cornbelt of Iowa and Nebraska. I had bought enough steers to ship a trainload out of Philip, South Dakota. Duff and I arrived in Philip on Friday as we planned to load and ship the cattle out on Saturday. We planned to stay all night in Philip.

One of the ranchers, A. R. McIlravy, was driving his steers, along with a couple of neighbors, on horseback. His ranch was about 15 miles north of Philip. Duff and I drove out to find the steers to see about when they would arrive in Philip.

As I recall it was a warm, windy and dusty day. In other words it was quite miserable. We met the steers and riders about 12 miles out and I got a really good idea.

I suggested to Duff that he relieve McIlravy on his horse and ride for a while, while Mac and I checked on another bunch of steers being driven in to Philip.

It was not easy to persuade Duff, but finally he consented. He had never ridden a good ranch horse and this would be an experience for him.

Mac and I drove off and started thinking what a great trick we were playing on Duff as we had no intention of coming back and didn't expect to see him until the steers came into the stockyards. We knew that 12 miles of riding and walking was too much for anyone not used to it.

When the steers finally arrived at the stockyards, Duff was leading his horse. He was showing signs of saddle sores and lots of windburn and sunburn. I had never seen Duff so mad in my life and he proceeded to tell us how terrible and how awful we were. It was a little more severe for him than we intended it to be.

I had the billing all lined up on the steers and there was plenty of help to load them on the railroad cars. After we had the cattle loaded we stopped at the 73 Bar in downtown Philip for a refresher or two. During our conversation someone suggested that we hold a spitting contest. Several of the old-time rank cowboys wanted in for the price of $20 each, winner-take-all. There was enough interest and somehow I was elected to be the referee and the judge of the contest.

The cowboys handed me $20 which qualified them for one spit. They lined up and one at a time spit at a one gallon coffee can about 15 feet away. Most of the men chewed Beechnut or Horseshoe chewing tobacco and that made a big splash in or around the coffee can. There were usually four or five contestants and I would have to say they were real professional spitters. This kind of contest was seldom seen anywhere, but it was fascinating.

There was a poster on the wall in the bar advertising a big dance in the small town of Cottonwood, about 13 miles west of Philip. They had a big old dance hall that had been there many years and it had a lot of notoriety for dances. Everyone from all over the country came to these dances on Saturday night.

Duff and I decided to go to the dance even though he was hurting from his ride earlier that day. When we got to the dance it was about ready to start. Everyone was in a glorious mood. Most of the men wore open collared short sleeved shirts. That was the dress of the day. But Duff who was always a good dresser had on a white shirt and a blue tie. No other man in the building had on a tie — so I got another idea.

I had a good friend who always carried a jackknife in his pocket. I asked him to do something for me and the crowd. He said he would. I told him I wanted him to walk up to the man with the blue necktie, grab him by the tie and pull him over to him and cut the tie off short and throw it on the floor. Then just walk away.

He did as I asked and as he cut off the tie he said, "We don't wear ties in this town!"

That not only was a shock to Duff but to everyone in the dancehall. Then started the most amazing spectacle. Everyone started grabbing the shirt of the man next to him and tearing it to shreds. Everyone was laughing and joking and stripping shirts until no one was wearing a complete shirt. Some were torn to shreds and some were completely gone. No one got mad. It was a harmless free-for-all and everyone had a good time.

I'll always remember Duff. Even with all the grief and abuse I dealt him he always came back for more.

Chapter 14

Sutton Brothers

When I first came to South Dakota in the early 1930's and traveled all over the state, I found that the Sutton Brothers' (James, John and Raymond) livestock enterprises were talked about in all circles as being among the best in quality and volume and being among the best livestock operators in the entire state. They were famous for their purebred Hereford cattle, their large volume of quarter horses and draft horses that were second to none and their buffalo herd.

Edwin Sutton, father of John, James and Raymond, started in the purebred Hereford cattle business in 1914 when he purchased quite a number of registered cows.

Years ago farm and ranch work was done by man muscle and horse muscle. Every ranch needed good draft horses, so in 1916 Edwin started the family purebred horse business with five Percheron stallions. When tractors took over the farm and ranch work the need for draft horses declined, the family turned to a ranch-type horse, the purebred Quarter Horse. Sutton Quarter Horses have made it big on the race track, in the rodeo arena and the show ring.

Their buffalo herd was started in 1909 when Edwin Sutton traded some land for three buffalo cows and thereby establishing the oldest private buffalo herd in the nation.

They operated a beautiful ranch on the river bottom along the Missouri River north of Pierre. They also raised four or five hundred Hampshire pigs a year in the heavy timber along the Missouri River without any shelter other than the timber. The pigs were always wild but exceptionally thrifty.

Sutton Brothers developed one of the best herds of purebred Hereford cattle in the business. They bought the best registered cows they could find and developed the Sutton strain of Herefords. They also held great value for a superior bull. When you own the

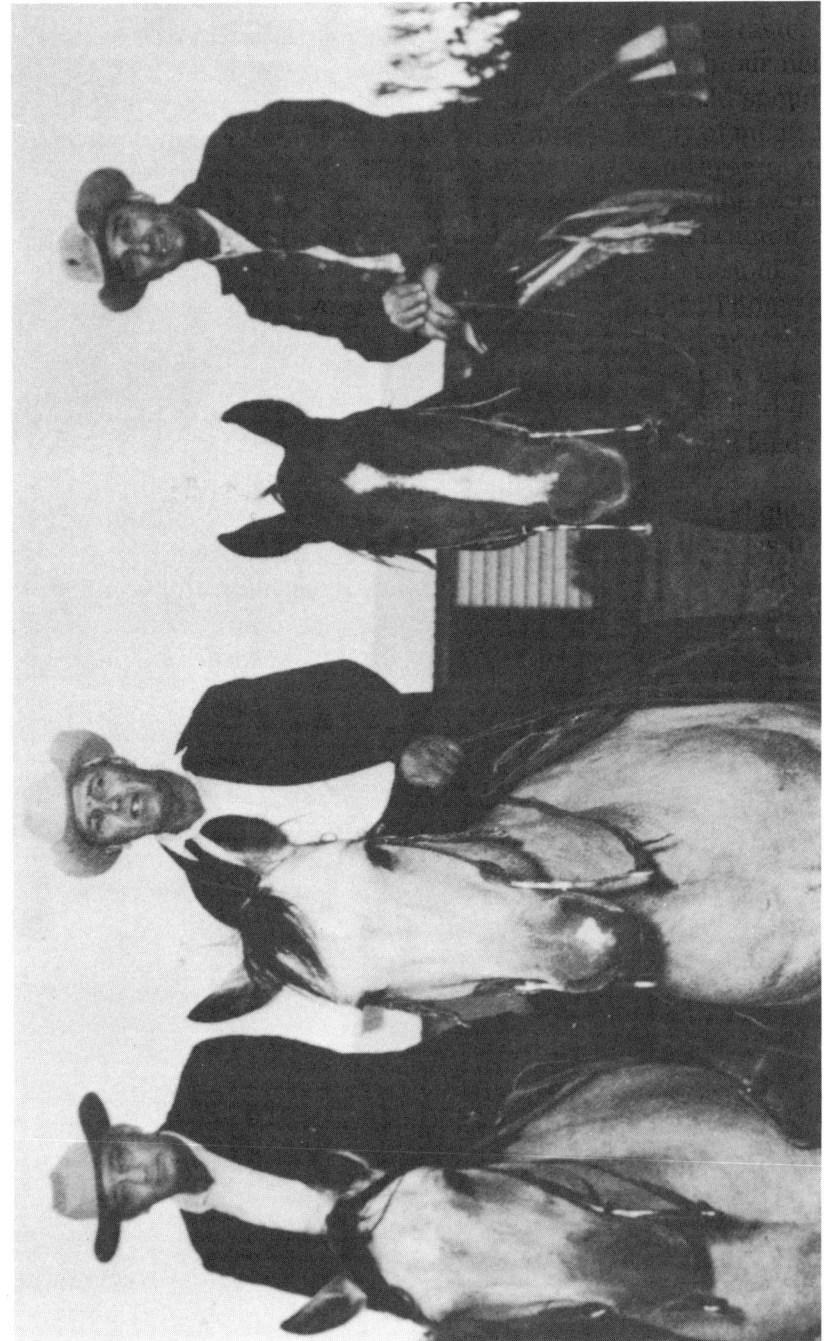

Sutton Brothers - James, John and Raymond

cows the best way to improve your off-spring is through the sire. They always had their eyes open for a superior sire. Price was secondary when they found a good potential prospect.

The Suttons natural ability to detect a top sire was a most important factor in their success in developing a volume herds of highly productive Hereford cattle, draft horses, quarter horses, bucking horses, buffalo and Hampshire hogs.

The volume bull sales held every spring were the barometer of all bulls sales in the country. People from many states came to their bulls sales. The first bull sale held at their ranch was in 1943 with Jim Magness as auctioneer. They built a new salebarn on the ranch in 1959.

Suttons also held horse sales and buffalo sales of big volume every year. People looked forward to their bull, horse and buffalo sales every year and attended in large numbers. There always seemed to be a magic about all Sutton sales. The buffalo sales always drew a large crowd as they were such a fantasy.

Feed crops were highly important to develop the volume of livestock raised on the ranch. Suttons had lots of land that was favorable to raise oats, wheat, corn, alfalfa and sorghum. They had

1945 - John Sutton with the stallion that was to become famous as a sire of bucking horses

many large fields up to two sections in size (1280 acres). The soil was excellent for farming and they raised lots of bumper crops over the years.

In the early 1950's the Army Corps of Engineers began building the Oahe Dam just north of Pierre for flood control along the Missouri River. The engineer's purchased the Sutton's eight thousand river bottom acres and they had until 1960 to move to higher ground. They moved some of the outbuildings up to higher ground, but the old ranch house that was home to all the Suttons and their families was torched in 1961 as the Oahe Reservoir waters crept up its steps. The flooding washed out the single-family system and the remaining home acres were divided into three nearly equal ranches.

The next generation of Sutton's that continued in the ranching business when the land was divided still run good outfits and have prospered.

Buffalo roaming the Sutton Ranch

Chapter 15

Ft. Dodge Serum Company

In 1939 or 1940 I was dealing in cattle all directions from the Missouri River when Ted called me one morning early from his home in Iowa. He asked me if I could find a couple thousand unvaccinated pigs for immediate delivery. He said that the Ft. Dodge Serum Company had called him wondering if we could find pigs weighing from eighty to one hundred forty pounds that had never been vaccinated. There had been a big outbreak of hog cholera all over Iowa and they wanted pigs right now or as soon as possible - the price was secondary - they would pay whatever it took to buy them. The supply of cholera vaccine had been exhausted and they needed the unvaccinated pigs to make more vaccine.

I told Ted I would change my route that day and go where I knew there were lots of pigs that ran wild in the timber along the Missouri River. They would be thrifty and good quality. The pigs raised in the river timber were always thrifty as they fed on self-feeders of grain, rabbits and whatever they could find to eat along the river.

I went north of Pierre to the Sutton Brothers ranch and found they had four or five hundred belted Hampshire pigs - one like the other. Their quality would suit anyone. They had been farrowed in April and May without assistance right in the timber along the river and had never been vaccinated for anything. Just what the Ft. Dodge Serum Company wanted.

I made a deal with the Sutton Brothers to buy the pigs on the per head basis so we didn't need to weigh them. The pigs were to be counted and loaded right in the timber on 14' bob-tailed trucks and 28' straight semis. The trucks would be there the next day as we needed to ship the pigs right away to the Ft. Dodge Serum Company in Iowa.

Suttons had woven wire catch pens along one side of the timber. The pigs seldom saw a man and were as wild as deer. I had seen a lot of wild west rodeos and cattle gatherings of much magnitude but never to the wildness of the gathering of these Sutton pigs. They would run and turn and squeal and snort and jump in all directions and some would get away with no chance of getting them back. It took a bunch of men on saddle horses to gather them and chase them into the catch pens.

We talked to the Suttons about more pigs and they said almost everyone along the river had pigs. So I went on up the river and found many more similar pigs - most belted Hampshires. They were willing to sell them for what we had paid Suttons.

If my memory serves me correctly the pigs weighed about one hundred pounds and we paid from $5.00 to $6.00 a piece for them. They were all belted Hampshires, except one group was Duroc Reds - but color or breed mattered not - they just needed to be thrifty unvaccinated pigs from eighty to one hundred forty pounds in weight.

The pigs all arrived in Ft. Dodge in excellent condition. The Ft. Dodge Serum Company head man complimented us on the quickness of the delivery of over two thousand pigs that he termed as an excellent string of pigs. He allowed us an extraordinary profit. And yes, we are still friends today!

Chapter 16

Jim Magness
The Master Auctioneer

Jim Magness was among the most influential men of my life. He was without question one of the most potent auctioneers I have ever experienced, even the auctioneers of today. His mannerisms and speech were most impressive. His dress was always appropriate and outstanding.

In everyday conversations or in the auction ring he had the ability to captivate the people. He was not just a salesman of the product but a salesman to the people.

Jim Magness at his home - 1943 - Note Clayton Jennings' picture on the piano.

Jim was the leading auctioneer at all the large Hereford bull and female sales in the area, including Knipplings, Suttons, Bones, Houcks and many others.

Soon after I met Jim in the mid 1930's I was aware that he was one of the most powerful Democratic politicians in the state. For a number of years he was chairman of the Democratic Party. He moved and changed a lot of people.

Jim and I developed a real meaningful friendship and eventually formed a business partnership.

Sale barns were just starting to develop over the western United States as a means to merchandise livestock of all kinds. The Miller City Council approached Jim and I as the ones to start and manage a livestock sale and bring much business to the city of Miller. After thorough study Jim and I decided to take over this project, which up to then had been in its infancy. We presented a proposal to the City and they accepted it.

With lots of help from people of all kinds we made this sale workable in a few months even though times were tough. The first sale was held July 20th, 1939, and from then on it was a big success. The seats were full of buyers and the yards were full of livestock at every sale. It developed into one of the newest and best livestock sales in the state and kept growing each year.

I enlisted in the Navy in 1942 and served until 1945. My brother Ted carried on the business so I had something to come back to after the war.

One day after I had been back from the Navy and at work again at the sale barn, Jim called me into our office and said, "Clayton, I want to run you for governor of South Dakota."

He was very sincere and sure that I could be elected governor. I thanked him for the confidence he had in me, but I told him I had no desire to be in politics. My desire was to be in land and livestock. This was probably the greatest compliment I had ever had.

The sale barn continued to flourish and consumed all our time. Jim wanted out as he had all the other sales he could handle. Ted and I wanted to put more time into the ranching business, so we sold the sale barn in the early 1950's. Jim went his way and I went another.

Jim and I had a good and successful friendship and we remained personal friends the rest of his days.

The Miller Sale Barn, Miller, SD - 1940

Chapter 17

Rawhide

In 1940 I was living at the Brown Hotel in Miller, South Dakota. I was going to the country buying and selling cattle and promoting the new Miller Livestock Sale Barn that was owned by the Jennings Brothers (my brother Ted and me) and Jim Magness.

I had taken particular liking to kids who were trying to grow up. I gave them jobs helping me on some work projects at the salebarn. Most of the kids started when they were from eight to ten years old. They were eager to earn a little bit of money. It reminded me so much of when I was their age and I wanted to make a little money of my own. I never turned a kid down who wanted to work. Sometimes I had more kids than I had jobs, but I found something for them to do. There were always cattle that needed hay. The boys could always drag hay bales - as many as wanted to work - all over

Alfred "Rawhide" Meyer - July 1942

1942 - In front of the salebarn cafe. L to R - John Dixon, Geo. Engel, ? , ? , Pete Knapp, Bud Palon, ? , ? , Bea Newell, Jim Magness, Emma Palon, Betty Palon, Ted Jennings, Mary Knapp, Dr. Sessions, Jack Clement wearing white hat in back, Rawhide Meyer, the kid in front

the salebarn yards to the pens of cattle. We had bale hooks for the boys - they would thrust them into a bale and drag or carry them from the stacks, down the alley, in a gate to the feed rack in the pens. This was a real struggle for the small boys, but they never complained and never gave up. Sometimes they would have to stop and get their breath, then go on. This was the day of the Allis Chalmers round hay baler and the bales weighed from forty to fifty pounds.

We usually started new boys out picking up trash and the glass pop bottles from under the bleachers.(There were no pop cans in those days.) The boys could get two cents for each bottle. Depending on the size of the sale, two boys working together could earn from twenty cents to a buck.

The bigger boys graduated to a higher level of jobs. One of their favorites was using a long whip to whip the cattle down the alleys to the salebarn ring. Then they went back down the alley for another bunch of cattle - this was constant. Another group of boys would whip the cattle off the scale to the buyer pens. They got great joy out of snapping the whip which made a lot of noise. The level of wages may not have increased but it was more fascinating to the boys. I can't recall paying any kids over a dollar, even for a big sale - which would start at noon and run until late in the evening, and a few times until daylight the next morning. Some days the work was miserable as there would be rain, mud, snow or manure that splashed over ever inch of the boys, but you never heard a kid complain. During a long sale these boys must have traveled five or six miles down the alleys - not much wages but a lot of fulfillment. Some of the boys who come to mind are the Rosemores, the Kindles, Gary Gabriel, John Gerlach, Rawhide Meyer, but there were many many more whose names have slipped my mind.

There was always one or two young boys going with me in my car when I went to the country. Alfred "Rawhide" Meyer was one of the boys who seemed to look me up every day. He knew my car and if I wasn't in it he just got in and waited for me. I was always glad to see him. He was about ten years old when I took him on the first trip. He was quite a boy. He was a freckle faced, sandy haired kid and seldom did he have more than a grin or slight smile. He definitely was not loud or boisterous like most boys of that age. His willingness to do or try anything was exceptional. He had a pleasant disposition and it always felt good to have him around. It was very evident from the first time I met him that he had a lot of sincerity and loyalty. He always seemed to be waiting for me at my car. If he couldn't find my car he'd wait for me at the salebarn. He just knew I would come by sooner or later.

On one occasion when Rawhide was with me I was trying to sell a big black bald-faced horse to a gentleman who had shown some interest in the horse. Rawhide fixed my career as a horse-trader when he piped up with, "That run-away SOB!" The lecture Rawhide received following that statement is still fresh in his mind. I assured him that during horse-trading truth was not a requirement; all other times honesty was required but not as a horse-trader.

In the fall of 1940 I planned a cattle buying trip through western South Dakota. It would take several days. I always liked to have company with me when I made such a trip as it made things more pleasant and not so much drudgery of driving. Someone to visit with would break up the monotony of the trip.

I asked Rawhide if he would like to make this trip. He was all for it. I told him he would have to talk to his folks and let me know if it would be okay for him to be gone several days. I was going to leave early Monday morning and hoped to be back Saturday night. Rawhide's folks did let me know. They thought the trip would be good for Rawhide as he hadn't been out of the county. They hoped I could get along really well with him. I knew I would enjoy him! I never realized how well acquainted I could get with a ten year old kid on a five day trip.

We arranged to leave early the next morning as we had a lot of miles to travel. Rawhide was waiting for me at the Hotel when I came out of my room.

We drove south from Miller and headed for Chamberlain, where we would cross the Missouri River. On the way I thought I should enlighten Rawhide somewhat on what to expect on the trip and for him to be sure and remind me to get a "survival kit" before we crossed the river at Chamberlain. Rawhide asked, "What the heck is a survival kit." His word "heck" was the first word of slang I had heard from him. I told him a survival kit was something to drink and some food, so we could survive in case of an accident or some bad weather that might stall us for hours, a day or two, until we could get back to civilization.

I told Rawhide about the first time that I crossed the Missouri River at Ft. Pierre, South Dakota. I hadn't thought of anything to eat, but when you get west of Ft. Pierre the ranches are vast and far between. There are more coyotes, prairie dogs and rattlesnakes by far than people. If you had trouble you would have to walk a long distance to find any livelihood. It would be a long tough day and you would find out what real hunger was. I was about eighty to a hundred miles northwest of Ft. Pierre. I had dealt on some cattle and was headed back to Ft. Pierre on a gumbo trail, no road what-so-ever. This was late afternoon and a big black cloud came up and it rained steadily. This gumbo soil gets heavy and thick and sticky. It rolled up under my wheels and I could not make my car go an inch further. I was really stuck and it was already getting dark. I realized I was in a real mess and couldn't do a thing about it. I was as hungry as a bear and had nothing to eat in the car. I wondered if I could walk either north or south to the highway. I didn't make it more than five yards from my car and the heavy gumbo stuck to my boots making it almost impossible for me to move. I got back to my car. I got in the back seat, I couldn't sleep so I did a lot of thinking about starving to death. All night long I heard the coyotes howl. It was real spooky.

A rancher on a tractor came along the next morning. He was a fellow of whom I had bought cattle. He just laughed at me when he saw the predicament I was in. He did hook onto my car with a chain and pulled me out to Highway 14 where I used my tire iron to dig the gumbo out from around my wheels so they would turn and I could get to town. I limped into a gas station in Ft. Pierre where I gassed up and washed off a ton or more of gumbo.

I said to Rawhide, "Now you know what a "survival kit" means!"

We traveled south from Miller. As we drove down the main-street of Chamberlain, Rawhide suddenly shouted, "Whoa, we can get the survival kit right at that store." We stopped and went into the store. I asked him to help me pick up enough grub to last a couple of days. We decided some pop was most important, so we got six bottles of 7-Up, a box of saltine crackers, some sugar coated doughnuts and three or four kinds of cheese. I intentionally slipped in a packet of Limburger cheese - I never was able to stand it but I wanted to test Rawhide.

We came to the bridge crossing the Missouri River. I pulled out a small shirtpocket sized notebook and a pencil. I always carried some notebooks and extra pencils with me in the car. I gave the notebook and pencil to Rawhide and said, "Rawhide, I want you to make a notation of every river we cross on this trip. I want you to be able to spell and enunciate the name correctly and know its geographical location. I also want you to be able to tell me what direction the river is flowing and what it dumps into." I always required a lot of Rawhide and he never disappointed me. He was eager to do what I asked.

We stopped on the middle of the bridge. It was early in the morning and there was no traffic coming from either direction, so I defied the law for a couple or three minutes. I said "Rawhide, here is your first river." He got his pad and pencil in operation and made some notations. We drove on across the bridge into the ranch country where we were going to look at and try to buy some cattle. We were also going to try to convince the ranchers to consign their cattle or horses or sheep to the new Miller Livestock Auction Barn.

We stopped at numerous ranches between river crossings where we had commitments to look at the cattle they had for sale. During the trip we bought a trainload of cattle to be shipped within a ten day period and the ranchers were to deliver them to the railroad we designated in their area. I was buying the calves in 1940 for $40 to $45 a head. Rawhide asked me why I paid some ranchers $40 and some ranchers $45. Right then he got a lesson in cattle buying. I told him what to watch for - weight, size, conformation of herd, color, compactness, etc etc. After that I quizzed him on each rancher's herd. (Rawhide told me that even today, over fifty years later, he never looks at a herd of cows and calves today without going through the whole process.)

We put in long hours from early in the morning until after dark. When Rawhide got tired he would crawl in the backseat of my car for a good nap. If I had some business with a rancher late in the evening Rawhide would sleep in my backseat. He was always there. I never worried.

During all our travels Rawhide was alertly watching for every bridge that had a river running under it, so he could get the name down properly (the rivers all had their names on signs near the bridges). The first river we crossed after the Missouri was the White River near the town of White River. We drove across the bridge where I stopped the car and we walked back to the center of the bridge. We observed the river in both directions. He wrote down the location and description of the land. We walked back to the car and continued our business of buying cattle. Rawhide always kept busy memorizing what he had written down on his notepad.

We planned to spend the first night in Philip. We headed northwest from White River. As we neared Philip we crossed the Bad River. This time when we reached the bridge I dropped Rawhide off so he could walk all the way across the bridge. This gave him time to think and do what I had asked. I drove across and waited for him on the other side. He carefully observed the river both ways, made his notations on his notepad, walked to the car and we continued into Philip.

Early the next morning we left Philip and headed northwest. We wanted to reach Belle Fourche by nightfall as we planned to stay there. We continued to stop at ranches buying more cattle. Late in the warm afternoon the Limburger cheese developed such an odor that it was too much even for me. Before I tossed it out I asked Rawhide to take a taste of it which he did - he grimaced somewhat, shook his head and said, "Clayton, I don't like that stuff." We threw it into a creek bottom as we went by. We both agreed it was a horrible odor. As we neared our destination we crossed the next river. It was the Belle Fourche River. Rawhide went through the same procedure and once again we continued on into Belle Fourche.

We left Belle Fourche before daylight, this time heading east as we planned to spend the night in Eagle Butte. We stopped at numerous ranches but did not cross any rivers that day. When we left Eagle Butte the next morning we headed north, planning to spend the night in McLaughlin. We crossed the Moreau River which is a very beautiful river with many miles of grazing on the meadow lands on both sides of the river. The next river we crossed before reaching McLaughlin was the Grand River. Rawhide continued his ritual at each river.

The next day we headed south toward Ft. Pierre and the end of our journey. We crossed some of the same rivers we had crossed earlier on our trip. We continued to stop at numerous ranches. One of these was the Earl Sonnenshein Ranch sixty miles from Ft. Pierre in no man's land at the mouth of the Cheyenne River. Earl was my best big friend in that day and Rawhide was my best little friend and I had the two of them together way up on the Cheyenne River.

As we traveled from ranch to ranch, I had another dream! I wanted Rawhide to be dressed western like the rest of the cow-

1940 - Clayton Jennings, Rawhide Meyer, and Earl Sonnenshien at Dr. Pangburn's farm near Miller, SD

Fischer Bros. Merchantile Store, Ft. Pierre, SD

boys. If he fulfilled all of his assignments that I gave him on the trip and did a good job of it, I would dress him just like me.

He had everything down to perfection! He did an excellent job! He knew every river, where they were located and their terrain! So when we pulled into Ft. Pierre we stopped at Fischer Brothers Mercantile Store. Rawhide and I went into the store. Antone Fischer greeted us. I said, "Antone, you fit this boy up with everything from head to toe. Make it the best you have." It was a real pleasure seeing Antone outfit him with everything from hat, shirt, Levis, underwear, socks and jacket to a pair of Nocona boots. This was Rawhide's first pair of boots. He was so proud.

My rewards were great as I watched this process and Rawhide's expressions.

Rawhide is a classic example of a poor boy from a small town making good. He was born at the beginning of the "Dirty Thirties" into a large family. They were poor, as were most all families of that era and area, but that did not stop him!

Rawhide was graduated from Oregon State University in 1959 with a BA in Forest Management-Ecology with a minor in Wildlife and a minor in Business Adminstration. He went to work for the Forest Service as a Forester. In 1962 the Forest Service sent him back to get his masters in Range Management-Range Ecology. After receiving his Masters the Forest Service assigned him to northeast Oregon. He has retired after 32 years of Forest Service Resource

At Wildhorse Symposium on Bear Valley Ranger Dist. - standing in one of the wild horse traps. Al Meyer center talking to chief of forest service, legislators, ass't Sec. of Agriculture and entourage

Al Meyer, District Ranger - 1st National Wildhorse Symposium 1980 - Wild Horse Annie in background

Rita and Al Meyer - 1995

Management at John Day, Oregon. He still does some consulting work if he feels good and wants a few extra bucks.

I feel that our trip through western South Dakota was the beginning of a journey Rawhide followed all through his life.

Chapter 18

Navy Fighting and Fun

When the Japanese bombed Pearl Harbor on December 7, 1941, the United States entered World War II by declaring war on Japan.

In April, 1942, instead of waiting to be drafted I decided to enlist in the Navy. I went through boot camp in San Diego and aviation ordinance school in Seattle. In August 1942 I was sent to the South Sea Islands spending the next 16 months on New Georgia and Emirau. Originally when we left the States we were informed that our stay in the South Pacific would be no longer than 6 months because of the conditions. It was all jungle — hot and humid and lots of mosquitoes.

The following are three letters I wrote home to family and friends.

The first, to my banker Art Cahalan, was written when the Japanese were keeping us mighty busy.

The next two were written after the fighting had lessened and we had a chance for some recreation without the fear of the Japanese bombers flying over.

Clayton Jennings and his dad and mother - 1944

NAVY LIFE

Somewhere, Southwest Pacific
June 28, 1943

Friend Art:
Received today yours of May 11 and let me say every letter is a grand consolation for us. I can't reveal exactly where we are but in view of the fact it took your good letter via regular mail 47 days to reach me, you will know I am a mighty long way from the U. S. - also that where we are, there is no pleasure cruising, but definitely in the theatre of war of the Southwest Pacific. However I have had air mail letters in as few as 13 days from date of post mark, but 20 days seems to be the approximate average time for air mail deliveries.

I regret I can't relate some of my specific experiences to date, but I can tell you in general terms a few things that may interest you.

We are living on an island about half of which is a coconut plantation and the other half real tropical jungle. There are thousands of beautiful and heavy producing coconut trees aligned in slightly curved rows about 20 feet apart and miles long. Of course, now the plantation is inactive so the ground is littered with coconuts from ever bearing trees. Coconuts quite frequently fall with a heavy thud and right now I am sitting directly under a coconut tree with approximately 60 well matured coconuts waiting for a little breeze to detach them, so if you find an ink splash somewhere from here on you will know there was a direct hit on me.

The sun is quite intense so we wear the lightest and most comfortable garb during the day. A typical garb is a pair of shorts and shoes and socks. The evenings cool off reasonably well from the breeze off the sea (just now one of those coconuts fell and cracked the windshield on a jeep just four feet from me) so we put on long trousers and long sleeve shirts for protection against mosquitos.

The beaches here are all lined with coral formation so that prevents us from a daily swim. However, we do go out on boats and have a fine swim in about 30 feet of water that is crystal clear. It is so clear that we can see all the spectacular coral formations with all its beautiful blended colors. One can see innumerable tropical fish of all sizes, colors and combination of colors and beauties beyond imagination. Shakers and barracuda are often sighted, which means the end of our swimming party.

We have several hundred native cattle here and from what information I can get they were brought on the island by plantation owners. They are of inferior quality and show considerable inbreeding. They seem to be a cross of all the dairy bred cattle I know of. They show definite traces of red polls, milking Shorthorn, Guernsey, Jersey, Swiss, Airshire and Holstein. Some show about half Brahma blood and I understand there is a big Brahma bull here on the island, but as yet I have not been able to find him. The grass here is sort of a bunch grass and grows thin on the ground below the coconut trees. It seems to have but little feed value, as the cattle as a whole are very thin. In fact, as thin as many Dakota cattle during the bad droughts. The cattle have a long narrow face, but I'd say that they have a right to have a sad mug with all that they have to contend with.

You no doubt have heard of fellows going "wacky" in isolated outposts. Our term for that state of mind is, "Well, he is counting his coconuts" - in as much as coconuts are so plentiful that they are valueless. So to prevent the

Airstrip on the South Sea Island of New Georgia

stage of "counting our coconuts" we develop hobbies to occupy our mind when we are not on duty, which is usually several hours in the evening. Some hobbies are - selecting pretty shells on the beach and making bracelets and necklaces, carving pipe bowls and novelties from rare species of hard wood found here on the island, gathering souvenirs, writing poetry, etc.

Here is a true story as it happened one night during an air raid. It was about 2 a.m. and we were huddled in our foxholes (special deluxe model). We had already experienced one salvo of bombs, several of which were so close that we could hear the shrieking, swishing noise as it fell before its impact and detonation. The earth around us trembled from the concussion of the explosion, of course, terrific anti-air-craft fire and search lights add lots of glamor if you can call it that. Let me say those are horror stricken, dramatic moments and not to be forgotten. On with the story - we were listening intently to the approaching drone of another wave of Mitzy-Bitzys (our term for Jap bombers). By the way, the Jap bombers are easily distinguishable from our bombers, as their motors have a peculiar purr similar to that of a washing machine. On with the story again. All of a sudden a big black man dives into the entrance of our foxhole. He was horror stricken and bewildered. He says "Gentlemen. would you kindly move over and make room for one poor peace lovin black man?" Naturally we crowded together and let "Bones" (call name) in. One of the boys said, "Bones, what is the matter with your foxhole?" Bones replied, "Why, one of dem black men in my foxhole insists on swearing something frightful. You gentlemen know dis am no time for swearin! Dis am de time for prayin!"

We all had quite a laugh over that but nevertheless it was most realistic of the occasion.

My personal health is good thanks to a rugged constitution. Hello to any and all the gang and special regards to all the bank force.

Sincerely,
s/s Clayton

P.S. I would enjoy hearing from you of the livestock and crop conditions. Send my best wishes and good luck to George and Art.

DEEP SEA FISHING

South West Pacific
December 19, 1943

Dear Ted and All,

I will attempt to relate my experiences on our first deep sea fishing party which took place a couple of weeks ago.

Eight of us fellows requested and were granted permission to go on an all day fishing party. We have a flat top boat that we rigged up from an old Jap schooner that had been captured. We had an old motor that had been taken out of service and the mechs overhauled it completely during their spare time. They installed the motor, a drive shaft and propeller screw. We remodeled the boat to suit the occasion we had in mind. The new stream-lined boat was 30 feet long, 12 feet wide, with a plain flat deck. The motor was secured down in the hatch below the water line. This was to be its maiden cruise.

We had 5 A. M. chow together, gathered up the fishing tackle and other necessary equipment, and secured some chow from the galley for a mid-day lunch. Of course, we took water canteens, and sun hats and shirts for protection against an intense sun. We "shoved off" about 6 A. M. and headed out where some natives had told us the fishing was good. There were a good many coral reefs interspersed in the water surrounding a bunch of little islands. We opened the motor to the limit and it made about 10 knots. The stern drew water within a foot of the deck so you can see we were practically level with the surface of the water. As we got well under way six of us dropped our lures with bright colored cloth streamers attached and let out 100 to 150 feet of 75 lb. test line. We cut the motor until we were making about 5 knots and of course the lures and lines streaming gently behind us—so the fishing was on. Only six of us fished at a time as it took two coxswains to navigate the boat. One operated the motor and the rudder and the other stayed up front on the bow to watch for shallow coral reefs upon which the boat can high center or cause a hole to be rammed in the bottom and possibly sink the boat. We sure didn't want to "abandon ship" in these shark infested waters. We had only two life jackets so it would have to be every one for himself, swim or else, in case of such a misfortune. We would take turns at the undesirable job of coxswain so everyone would have a fair chance. I can't give you the specific addresses of each of the boys so I will let their respective home states' represent each of them. They were Iowa, New York, California, Oregon, North Carolina, Arkansas, Tennessee and South Dakota.

We were out about an hour or about six miles when New York hooked a fish. He called out "strike", at which time the rest of us pulled in our lines, and cut the motor to idle, as a man with a catch rates the entire deck and all the sea as these deep sea fish put up a real battle and oftentimes entangle several lines and even go under the boat and on all sides. A battling fish may take the fisherman all around the deck before he is overcome and landed. The lines of the five of us were all in and we were watching enviously every move the fish and even the New Yorker was making. After a few minutes of struggling he got the catch up to where we could plainly see him in the clear blue water. He was a good sized fish and New Yorker called for a gaff, which is a metal hook on the end of about a six foot pole. It is used to hook the fish broadside and to land him so as to avoid snapping the line from a dead weight snap as the fish is hoisted from the water. The gaff hook was effective and a nice 10 lb. mackerel was landed. Immediately the motor was stepped up to five knots and the lines were let out again. Within a couple minutes Oregon called,"strike" and the same procedure took place and ended with the landing of about a 12 lb. tuna. We were under way again and the coxswain called out "good water" which meant an ideal place for fish. We were crossing a coral reef about 20 feet below the surface of the water. We had just passed over the edge of the reef and where the water was deep when four of the six lines had simultaneous "strikes", namely California, North Carolina, Arkansas and Tennessee. That was quite a spectacle to watch and when the occasion had finished they had landed four beautiful barracuda, ranging in weight from 8 to 12 lbs. This was quite an inspiration so we lost no time in getting underway again. We fished until about noon and caught several more fish. Several including myself, indicated desire for some food so we anchored out and set out the chow. We had quite a variety - U. S. Vienna wieners, bread of U. S. flour, Australian catsup and preserves, and New Zealand fruit. It didn't take long to appease our appetites and to get underway for more fishing. You notice that up to now Iowa and So. Dakota had not made a catch. However we had muffed a couple "strikes" and were the victims of wisecracks and embarrassment. We both caught fish soon after lunch and they proved to be the largest of the entire lot of fish so our prestige was partially restored. We caught several more fish and decided it was about time to start back to the base. We fished on the way back and caught several nice fish. We located a school of sea bass and caught several weighing 5 to 10 lbs. We were just about two miles from the base when Oregon caught a small one as he declared it to be as he was pulling him in. He had remarked that he wouldn't need the gaff to land this one. We were all watching from the stern and when the fish had been maneuvered up to within six feet of the boat a big sea bass gulped the catch and dived for deep water. The line being tight turned the monster over on his side against the boat. The impact alone with the tremendous jerk on the line nearly jerked Oregon into the water. We all had a plain vision of the big fish and all let out a barrage of oh's and ah's. Everyone was bewildered but as we gained the presence of mind we made suggestions of how to land him. We knew we couldn't land him by force so decided to let him have some line and try to wear him out. Two of the crew had Oregon by the britches to keep him from being jerked overboard. The rest of us stood ready with gaffs, rifles and pistols in case Oregon got him in sight again. Oregon gave him a real tussle for about ten minutes but finally he gave a terrific lung and snapped the line. This was a big disillusionment but we had fun while it lasted. We estimated the sea bass to weigh 200 lbs and some of the radicals estimated 300 lbs. Anyway, he was a dandy so we have sincetime nicknamed Oregon as SeaBass.

We came into the base with a catch of 21 fish, total weight of about 200 lbs, which we turned into the galley for a fish chow. We all had a swell time and one which we will long remember. To make the day a total success we found a jackpot of air mail letters waiting for us.

All is well here and I am feeling good. I'm brown as an Indian.

Love to all,
s/s Clayton

P.S. We have a league softball game tomorrow which will be our 4th game. We lost our first league game and won the next two. We got knocked all over the field in our first game. I guess we were over-confident. We had won five consecutive games prior to the league opening and we thought we had the hot club of the league. We looked bad in the first league game but since we have settled down and take each game seriously. I play third base and am hitting about 400.

You might send this epistle down to the folks if you think they would be interested. That would avoid my writing the same lingo.

Clayton Jennings and a buddy with some of their catch in the South Pacific.

Fishing party - John Wingenback, Happy Bass, John Dell, Bud Littleton, Ralph Hackett, Clayton Jennings and Victor Walberg

WILD BOAR HUNT

Sept. 1, 1943

Southwest Pacific

Another boy and I had a most interesting day just lately. We had a day off so went hunting "wild boar" in the jungle and I do mean jungle.

We have a two-man pontoon boat made from 2 surveyed aircraft auxiliary gas tanks and a couple of poles. We started out early one morning with a 45 calibre pistol each and plenty of ammunition - also a few rations, water canteen, and some trinkets to trade with the natives and a prayer. We told our buddies approximately where we were going and if we failed to get back to send a searching party out after us the next day.

So we started out early in the A. M. and paddled our way up the sea and coast line. After several hours of navigating we spotted a small island with dense jungle and a few coconut trees. We decided to explore so we paddled up to the shore and tied our rig to the coral and proceeded into the jungle. We had gone less than 100 yards when we spotted a wild pig that was evidently eating the remains of some coconuts which had been broken and eaten by some natives. He was a nice fat pig, just out of the weaning age and would weigh about 60 pounds. We were so surprised we froze in our tracks. We decided to give the word so we could fire simultaneously. The pig was only about 30 yards away and just as we cocked our 45's he heard us, pricked up his ears and stood broadside for a perfect shot. We both fired practically at the same time and one of us got a slug into him and crippled him so the chase was on. He took of through the jungle like a frightened deer and we were right after him blasting away at him with our 45's. We trailed him and shot at him for an hour but let me say it is damn hard to hit a wild pig with a 45 and running through the jungle. We lost track of him several times but jumped him up after a few minutes search. We thought we had him when we ran him into a corner or rather point of the island. My buddy had a standing broadside shot and did knock him completely into a tumble. He shouted to me that he "got him" but when we got to the spot the pig was gone and we saw him no more in spite of another hour of searching. We were damn weary and decided to get back to our boat and eat some chow and have a good drink of water. All the way we lamented because we had missed getting him and consequently missed having a "roast pig" for our whole crew.

It was well past noon when we took to the sea again. We spotted some natives in a canoe about a mile distant and raised our paddles and waved them in the air and they in turn did likewise to signify they were friendly. So we rowed together and had quite a chat as one of them talked a little English. They took quite a fancy to some of our trading stock so they invited us up to their village. We followed them up the coast winding around coral reefs and finally into their village. It was so hidden that it cannot be seen from over 50 yards at sea. They took us all through their huts and showed us all the family. You see they live in families from grandmother and grandfather on down to tiny babies. Grandmother was very old probably 75 to 85 years old. There were fathers, mothers, uncles, aunts and plenty of kids of all sizes. It was a sight we will never forget. They were amazed as much at seeing us as we were them. We had never seen things like that before. After looking over the huts etc. we traded for some nice souvenirs which I will mail to you as soon as we

get permission, which may be a while. We arrived home at dusk, tired and weary, but with a experience well worthwhile.
Love to all,
s/s Clayton

1943 - trading with the natives in the South Pacific

Chapter 19

My Golden Horses

During the late 1940's the northwestern part of South Dakota was suffering from drought conditions, which had existed for a couple of years. Many ranchers in that area were forced to sell all or part of their livestock because of the drought or their financial situation or both.

At this time the ranchers were using pickups and tractors and the demand for horses became nil in accordance with their past history. Every rancher had more horses than they needed and there was practically no sale. They let the horses run on the range and they were taking a toll on the grass. They were grubbing it off to a point where the ranchers were forced to do something. Get rid of the horses or sell the cattle.

It seemed as though every ranch where I went to buy cattle would try to sell me some or all of their horses. I turned down deal after deal of horses that were good. I had no idea how to merchandise them as horses were not in my line of business.

Then I had a dream that I followed. I could buy a band of mares with so little cost and I had plenty of room to pasture them at the Jack Cook ranch south of Ree Heights, South Dakota. I thought I would like to handle them just for the enjoyment I might get from them. I had no intention of making money!

One of the ranchers that I contacted about his cattle he had for sale told me that he had about 50 mares with 39 suckling colts at their side and 2 stallions, one about ten years old and the other one two years old. The stallions were running with the mares.

This rancher continuously asked me to buy his horses and wanted me to bid on them - that I refused to do. I told him if he wanted to put a price on them I would consider it.

It didn't take him long to say, "I want to sell them all and I'll take $20.00 a head for them." They were truly good saddle bred mares

Late 1940's - mares, colts and stud (on the far right) on the Cook Ranch

with a top set of sorrel and palomino colts on them, but they were ruining his ranch and not bringing in any dollars.

I gasped for breath on a price that was so cheap and when I came to I asked him, "What about the colts?"

And he quickly said "The colts have got to go with the mares as they belong with them until they are weaned. I will not ask you anything for the colts, but they have to go with the mares. I have the two palomino studs that I will sell at the same price as the mares."

I was almost in a state of complete shock at the price, so to keep from showing my hold card I didn't answer him yes or no, but said I would look at the cattle he had for sale.

We drove down into another pasture and looked at the cattle he had sorted off to sell. I could see that all his pastures were bare and could not support his horses and cattle.

I bought the cattle that he had for sale, for immediate delivery. We agreed on all the terms of the cattle deal, then we shook hands.

On the way back to the ranch he kept talking about the horses he needed to sell, and wished I would buy them from him. He wasn't aware that I surely was going to buy all the horses as I was playing difficult and hard to get on the horses. But I could see that the man was in real trouble trying to support his horses and cattle in such dry conditions. I developed considerable sympathy for him and his situation.

We rode back through the mares and colts and they were a beautiful sight and showed their breeding as quality saddle-bred mares.

I told the rancher that I didn't know what I was going to do with them as I wasn't in the horse business, but I was going to buy them all at the price he had asked.

On the way home I figured out how many trucks it would take to move them as soon as possible. I lined the trucks up for the next day. I told the rancher to pen the horses in one pen and the cattle I bought in another, as I would have the trucks there the next day - and that I did!

I heard the rancher breathe a sigh of relief as the last loaded truck pulled out of his ranch yard.

I sold the cattle right off the trucks to a good customer of mine for a decent profit - and they were gone.

I had the trucks take the horses to the Jack Cook Ranch six miles south of Ree Heights, South Dakota where I had a fresh pasture with good water for them. A couple months later when the colts were old enough to wean I took them off their mothers. I took them, five or six at a time, to the various salebarns in our area. I put them up for sale at the regular livestock sales at Miller, Huron, Redfield and Fort Pierre. At each sale I had them visible in separate, highly exposed pens, so people could see them when they walked toward the salebarn. The colts created a complete sensation at each sale. The people would be hanging on the fences to see the colts and the bidding was rapid fire. Some people bought two, usually a well matched pair in size, quality and color. They were bidding like there wasn't going to be any more colts! They brought from $17 to $34 dollars on colts that had in reality been given to me. I could hardly believe it. I was just trying to help a poor rancher out of a bad situation when I took the colts with their mothers.

I watched each sale and each time it stunned me to the bottom of my boots - I just couldn't believe it. This gave me a great feeling because I had a running jump on this horse endeavor, as I had not planned to make any money what-so-ever. I was beginning to like the saddlebred-type horses of which I knew nothing about until this deal. In Iowa as a kid growing up my dad had all draft horses. He taught me to feed, curry, harness and drive draft horses. They were all we had in the line of transportation and farming. The draft horses were nothing like these horses.

The colts were all gone and I realized more from their sale than the total cost of the entire herd when I bought them. We wintered the stallions that had been running with the mares in a couple of small pens where they could get in the barn for shelter. The mares were running in a fresh pasture with right good shelter. They wintered with just the grass and a salt lick, without supplemental feed what-so-ever, except when we had a snow and blow we pulled a hayrack full of good hay into the pasture and they could self feed on it.

The mares started foaling in early May. We had excellent luck winding up the foaling season with forty seven strong, thrifty and good colored colts, mostly palomino but some sorrel.

I made special effort all winter and summer to stop at the Cook Ranch to admire the mares and colts. I got to liking them so well that I decided that I would keep the mares and go into the horse business. These are desires that get to a man when he has a lot of good luck and fantasy.

There were a lot of ranchers in this territory who had heard about these horses. They would come to me and ask if I would show them the horses. Most indicated that they would like to buy a colt or two, which made me feel good.

In late summer a friend of mine Virg Smith came thru Miller. He stopped to visit Ted and me. Virg was from Algona, Iowa, and was a highly potent livestock man with considerable wealth.

Virg had heard of the band of mares and colts that I had. We visited about the horses and he wondered if I could take the time to show them to him, which I did! I loved to show off my horses!

The pasture was some over a section (640 acres) and had gently rolling hills with a creek running down the center. There were lots and lots of rocks on the higher ground, but none along the creek. I drove my car along the creek where there were no rocks. We went nearly to the far end of the pasture before we located the horses, which were mostly together. The horses put on what you would think was a performance. They strung out and came by us. They trotted or ran along the hillside, about fifty or sixty feet from us, nearly single file. They had their heads in the air and their tails flying behind them. I would say it was the most beautiful sight of horses you could ever see. The stallions were bringing up the rear. We followed them to the other end of the pasture. They turned around and performed the same as the first time. It was an eye-catching sight to behold! Virg was electrified. I could tell by his wordless expression. I could see that he truly liked these horses.

We were close to the gate, so I started to drive out of the pasture, but Virg said, "We're not done yet. I want one more look." We drove through the horses again and as we neared the gate he surprised me by asking me what I would take for all of them. I told him I did not have them for sale. I wanted to keep them to enjoy.

Virg came back with, "Clayton, I need about that many horses of these colors and kind. You can find more horses as you go along." I was aware that he had just shown me his hold card. He wanted them irregardless of price. Knowing that he wanted them so badly made me look at the realistic end of this horse deal. I let him do the talking, but I did answer any questions he had about the horses.

Smith was known as a big dealer in the livestock business. He kept saying to me, "Just price them all, at so many total dollars!" I knew I had to put up or shut up. I was trying to think of a magical figure in total dollars. It was definitely my turn. I quickly tried to come up with a total amount that wasn't ridiculous either way. This would include all the horses he had seen in the pasture - 50 mares, 47 colts and 2 stallions. I said " $21,000.00!" He was one of those guys who was quick on the trigger and he said, "Clayton, you have just sold the horses."

When I bought these horses I had no intention or thought of a profit. I felt that I had done a great favor for the rancher who needed to sell them and I would have a year or more of total enjoyment just watching them milling around in the pasture. But the way the deal turned out, owning them less than a year, I realized the largest margin of profit for volume of fifty head or more of livestock than ever before in my lifetime up to then!

Jack and Georgia Cook on the Cook Longhorn Ranch south of Ree Heights, SD with some of their Longhorn cattle (in the background is where my golden horses ran)

Longhorn cattle on the Cook Longhorn Ranch - 1993

PART III
1945 - 1964

The Hyland Angus Ranch was my home for the next eighteen years. Ted and I were very fortunate. We were able to buy land that blocked out solidly, much of it on the north and south sides of Highway 14 between Highmore and Ree Heights. It was an ideal location for a purebred cattle operation.

We applied major overhaul jobs on the buildings and fences on the all ranches as we purchased them which took several years. We used the scheme of white buildings with green asphalt shingled roofs and white corrals with black posts on all the ranches. This scheme became the trademark of the Jennings Brothers ranches.

The Hyland Angus Ranch was the first to inseminate beef cattle by the volume. The extensive use of AI allowed us to develop what was probably one of the most uniform sets of Angus cows that the industry as ever seen.

We proved our reputation as top breeders by competing and winning at the major livestock shows in America.

During my years on the Hyland Angus Ranch I was married twice and had three children. I married Dorothy Fish in October 1946 and we had a son and a daughter, Charles Clayton and Gloria Jean. We divorced in 1956. In March 1959 I married Eloise Dwyer and we had one son, James Ted.

In 1962 Ted and I divided our partnership. Ted kept the commercial cattle and I kept the purebred cattle. We divided the land on the Hand/Hyde county line. Ted kept the Hand County land and I kept the Hyde County land.

In 1964 I sold my purebred Angus operation to Ankony Angus Corporation of New York.

Chapter 20

Hyland Angus Ranch

In 1945 the land buys in South Dakota looked so good to Ted and me that we decided to buy land and develop a big purebred Angus operation. There was more land for sale than ever had been before in South Dakota history, so the opportunity was there.

We wanted land in a good location as it is highly important for the ranch to be accessible at all times preferably on or near a hard surfaced road.

We were very fortunate to buy acres of land from 1945 to 1960 from $5 to $40 an acre. Much of this land was along Highway 14 between Highmore and Ree Heights, South Dakota. The land blocked out solidly and was an ideal location for a purebred herd. We kept putting ranches together. We'd sell or trade land if we found something we liked better or it fit our program better. At our peak we had about 40,000 acres of land.

We selected the name Hyland Angus Ranch because the town of Highmore was the highest point on the Chicago and Northwestern Railroad between Chicago and the Black Hills. We changed it to Hy and added land. So it became the Hyland Angus Ranch.

We applied major overhaul jobs on all the buildings and fences on all the ranches which took several years. We used the scheme of white buildings with green asphalt shingled roofs and white corrals with black posts on all the ranches. This scheme became the trademark of the Jennings Brothers' ranches. We hired a crew of three to five men to do this work during the summers, and it was seldom we didn't have a crew working on one part of the ranch or another. We completely renovated all corrals, so we had good working facilities on each ranch.

The Jennings Brothers' trademark wasn't just white buildings with green roofs, but good clean ranches with nothing strewn about, hard working people who respected each other and good Angus cattle.

We decided to raise Angus cattle as we had many friends in Iowa who preferred to feed Angus because of their efficiency and beef merit. The first Angus we bought were at an estate sale in Morley, Iowa. They were all registered Bell Boy breeding and we bought the herd in its entirety — probably 150 head total. They did so well for us that we didn't want anything but Angus. We continued to buy and raise good Angus cattle until our herd numbered 12,000 cows.

The Hyland Angus Ranch was the first outfit to artificially inseminate beef cattle, by volume. We started in 1955. AI gave us the benefit of a tighter calf crop (71% were on the ground within three weeks), better prices because of uniformity and quality, and the use of the best bulls of the breed.

Headquarters Ranch before the buildings were painted white — home of Clayton Jennings for 18 years

Hyland Angus Ranch home of Jim Blair and family

Hyland Angus Bull Ranch - home of Bud Hahn and family

Hyland Angus Ranch - home of Ernest Suhn, Jr. and family

Another set of excellent improvements on the Hyland Angus Ranch

October 1953 - Hyland Angus Ranch during the round-up of their calf crop. Confucius Joe, Harold Fritzel, Trail's End Ranch of DeSmet, SD, Dick Hahne, Journal Editor

Cows and calves on the Hyland Angus Ranch (1950's). Stock dam and self-feeder in the distance

Cows and calves on the alfalfa flats on the Hyland Angus Ranch (1950's)

Cows and calves near Elm Creek on the Hyland Angus Ranch. Elm Creek - a snake-like creek with lots of small tree cover

Phil Hazard and Clayton Jennings of Hyland Angus Ranch, Maurice Boney, Angus Journal Rep. 57 registered Angus bull calves that are going to the Frank Bosler commercial herd near Laramie, Wyoming

Roger Haberling, Dr. Vince DeRouchey and Randy Forman of Merriweather Veterinary Supply, Miller SD, preg checking an Angus heifer. Dr. Vince did a lot of veterinary work for a lot of years for the Hyland Angus Ranch

Chapter 21

Hyland Angus Ranch Crew

A RANCH IS NO MORE OR NO LESS THAN THE MEN WHO WORK FOR IT!

The Hyland Angus Ranch crew as a whole was the most capable and loyal as any crew ever to work on a ranch. These men and women were professionals in their line of work and never once could I question their decisions. Their sincerity and honesty made it possible for the Hyland Angus Ranch to be prominent in the Angus cattle business for many years.

We gave our men an extra incentive by making them feel a part of the Hyland Angus Ranch. We paid a good wage with bonuses being optional to us in accordance with the financial status of the ranch. Each family was furnished with a modern home with the operator being responsible for the upkeep of the place. We furnished each family with prime beef the year around by maintaining a small feed yard at one of the ranches for the development of fat cattle for slaughter. They had no need to tell us when they needed beef. They could get one for slaughter either on the place or at the locker plant in town. We also offered them a garden with the use of our equipment at no cost to them. Everyone was eligible for a few days off at a time but it would be arranged when there was no real important cattle situation planned.

Our ranch hands always worked for our interest and were loyal in all respects. They never kept track of their hours and many days were long and hard, especially during haying season or calving season.

The women held up their part of the deal by cooking for the whole crew whenever necessary. We always found jobs for any of the families who had children old enough to work.

We felt we were giving our hands an opportunity and many of them stayed with us twenty, thirty or more years.

1950's - James Krick, Bill Pender, Ernest Suhn, Jr., James and Bill McKown. Hyland Angus cattle in the background

1955 - Charlie Jennings on Thunder, Argyl Conner, Jim Hupp, Jack Cordell, Ernest Suhn, Jr., Jim Blair, Harold Wulf, Bob Fratzke, Keith DeRouchy and Jack Engle

1964 - Melvin Fischer, Allen Hanson, Ernest "Bud" Hahn, Harold Parlin, James Palon and Dean Henson

Chapter 22

Bull Sales at the Hyland Angus Ranch

The Hyland Angus Ranch started holding bull sales in 1953. The first two sales - 1953 & 1954 - were held at the Miller, South Dakota, sale barn.

In 1955 we held our first annual bull sale at the ranch. We had just completed a salebarn 36' x 144' with a 64' section forming the sale ring "T" at the east end of the building.

Our first sale at the ranch was very active and highly successful. It was just the beginning of many more sales to be held at the Hyland Angus Ranch.

We knew the demand and expansion of Angus cattle was just beginning. We knew that the Hyland Angus Ranch was but a small part in this great crusade, but we were greatly enthused by the challenge. We were determined to make available as many of the right kinds of bulls in the right condition as our operation could support.

Advertisement in the Angus Journal for the May 6, 1957 bull sale

May 7, 1955 - First bull sale at the Hyland Angus Ranch

Potential buyers before the bull sale at the Hyland Angus Ranch

1950's - bulls on the Hyland Angus Ranch

Angus bulls watering at a stock dam on the Hyland Angus Ranch (1950's)

Chapter 23

Hyland Angus Ranch Champions

In order for the Hyland Angus Ranch to establish a reputation as top breeders of Angus cattle, we felt we needed to compete and win at the major beef cattle shows and fairs in America.

Our cattle did exceptionally well in these competitions and this created more and better sales for us each year. We also made many connections with other Angus breeders through these shows and fairs that greatly enhanced our bull business which developed into a great bonanza.

1953 - Clayton and Dorothy Jennings, Russell Bucks and Phil Hazard with the First Prize Load of Junior Bull Calves at the National Western Stock Show, Denver, Colorado

1954 - ? , Ernest Suhn, Joe Pekarek, Marvin Fernow and Jim Hupp - First Prize Load and Reserve Champion Angus Bull Calves at the National Western Stock Show, Denver, Colorado

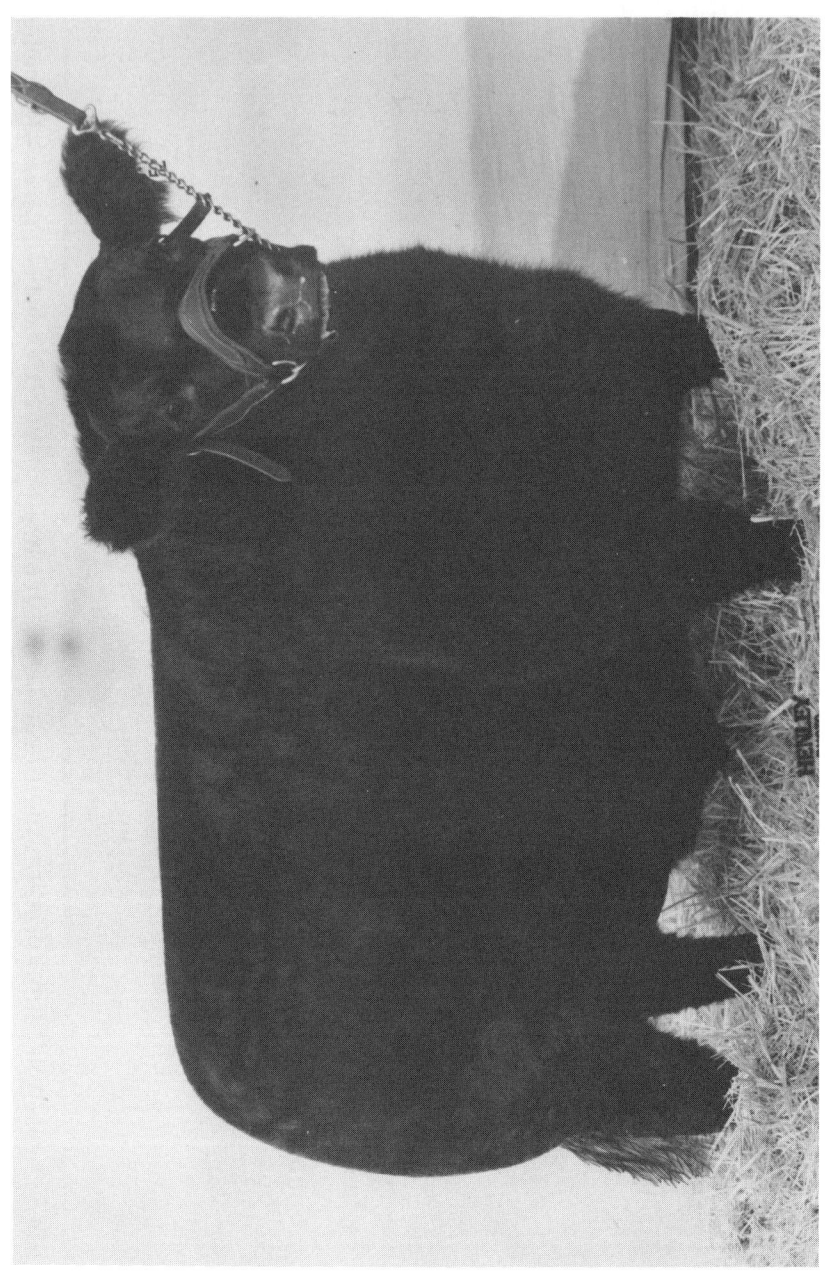

Hyland Black Jack, Reserve Grand Champion Steer and Champion Angus Steer, National Western Stock Show, Denver, Colorado

1955 - First Premium and Reserve Champion Junior Bull Calves — National Western, Denver, Colorado

1956 - Grand Champion Junior Bull Calves; Argyl Conner, ?, Clayton Jennings, Ross VanBalen, Jap Gadd, and Gordon Gadd, National Western Stock Show, Denver, Colorado

1956 - Grand Champion Junior Bull Calves; Clayton Jennings, Jap Gadd, Ross VanBalen, Argyl Conner on the fence, National Western Stock Show, Denver, Colorado

1956 - Grand Champion Junior Bull Calves, Argyl Conner & Clayton Jennings, National Western Stock Show, Denver, Colorado

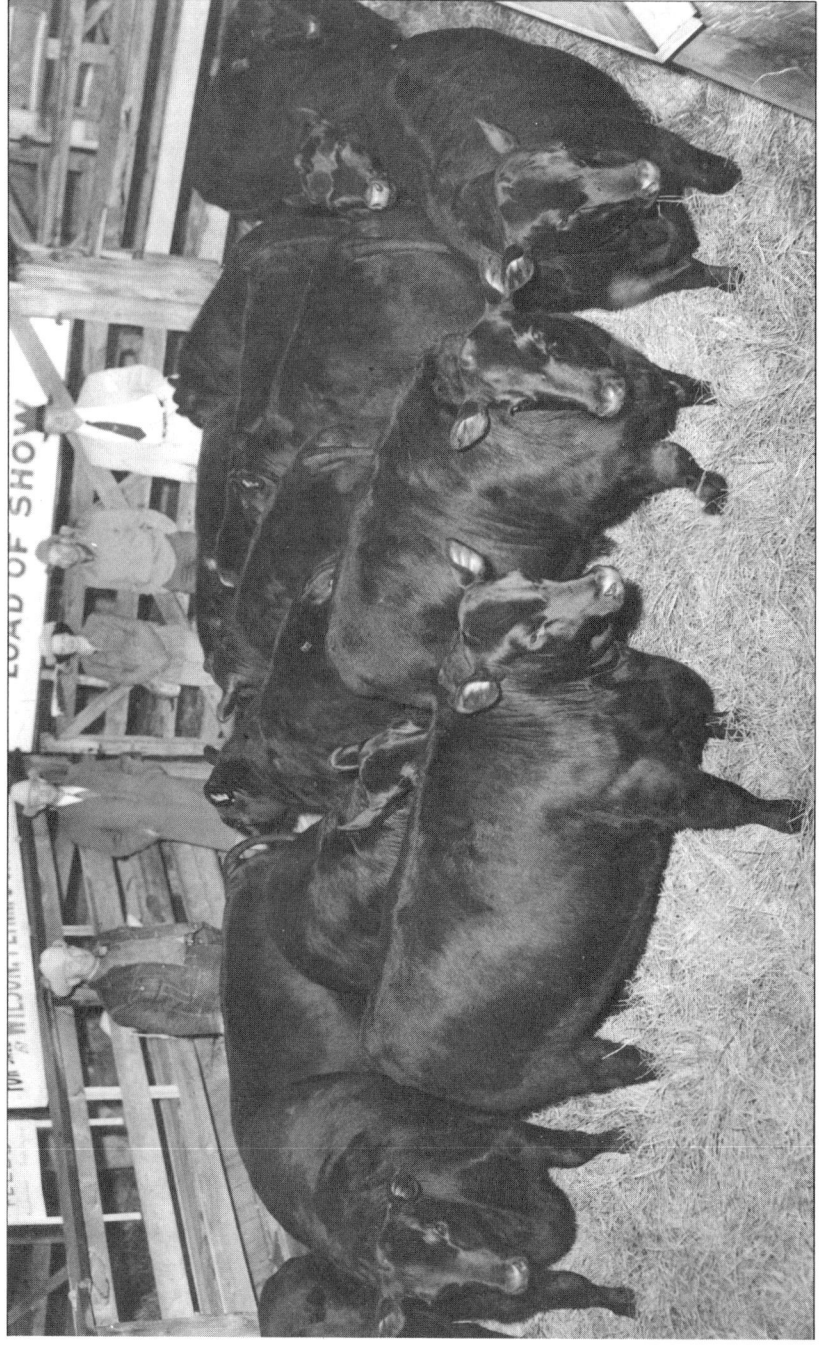

1951 - Kansas City Royal Grand Champion Steers. Bred by Jennings Brothers Hyland Angus Ranch, fed and shown by Russell Bucks, Davenport, Iowa. ? , Clayton Jennings, Dorothy Jennings, Russell Bucks, ?

1951 - Kansas City Royal Grand Champion Steers. Bred by Jennings Brother Hyland Angus Ranch; fed and shown by Russell Bucks, Davenport, Iowa. ? , Russell Bucks and Clayton Jennings

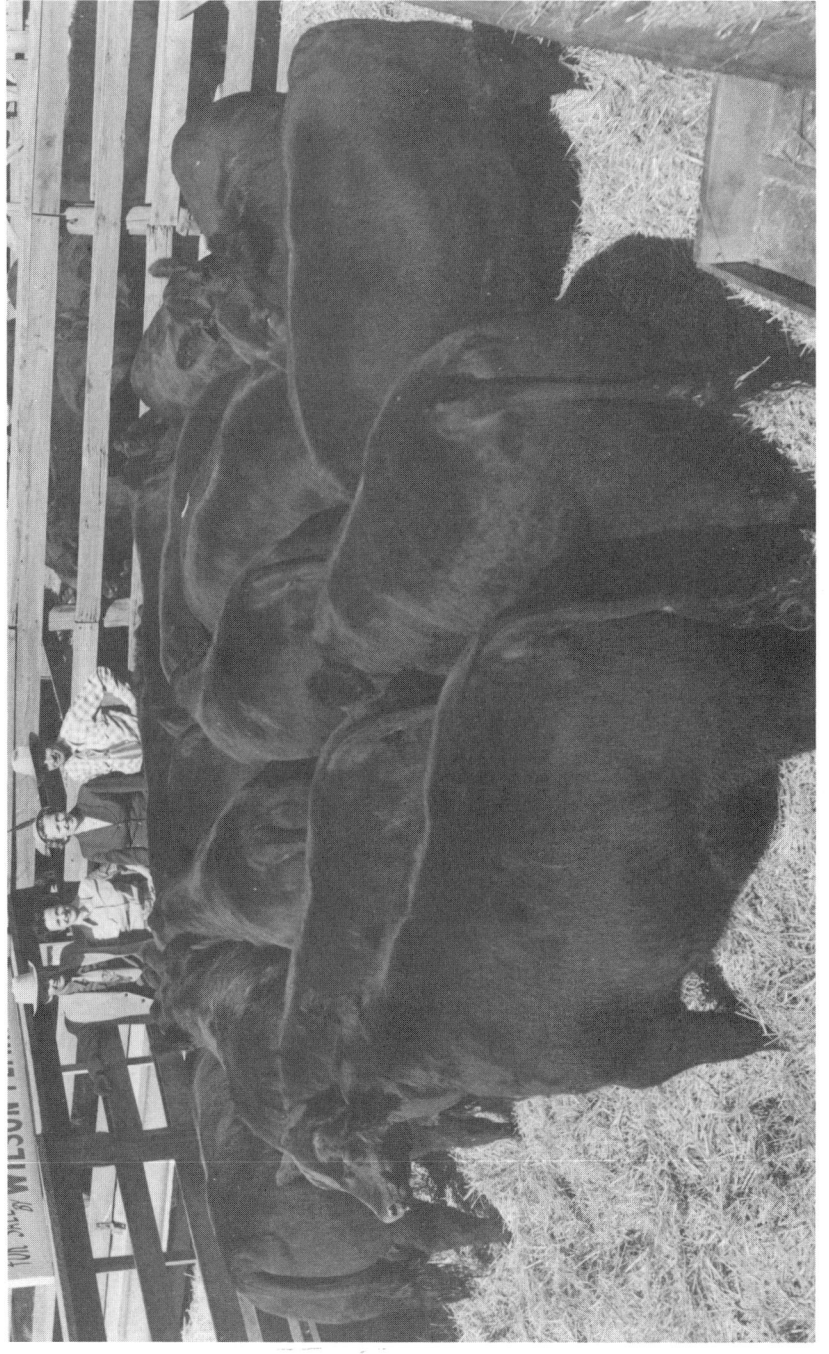

1952 - Kansas City Royal Grand Champions Steers. Bred by Jennings Brothers Hyland Angus Ranch and fed by Russell Bucks, Davenport, Iowa. Clayton & Dorothy Jennings, Mr. and Mrs. Russell Bucks

1953 - Great Western Livestock Show, Los Angeles, California. Grand Champion Carload Fat Steers. Bred by Jennings Brothers Hyland Angus Ranch; fed and shown by Karl and Jack Hoffman and Vern Joy, Ida Grove, Iowa

1953 - Chicago International, Chicago, Illinois. Reserve Champions of the Show and Champion Angus of the Show. Bred by Jennings Brothers Hyland Angus Ranch; fed and shown by Karl and Jack Hoffman and Vern Joy, Ida Grove, Iowa

1954 - Chicago International, Chicago, Illinois Grand Champions of the Show. Bred by Jennings Brothers Hyland Angus Ranch; fed and shown by Karl and Jack Hoffman, Ida Grove, Iowa

Late 50's, Chicago International Livestock Show at a gathering just prior to the Angus Show Awards Banquet. ?, Dale Runyon (glasses), Mr. Firpo from So. America, Lee Leachman, Dave Canning, John Momsen, Clayton Jennings, ?.

1953 - Eloise Jennings, Karl Hoffman, Clayton Jennings, L. M. "Doc" Cropsey. Grand Champion Angus Steers, National Western Stock Show, Denver, Colorado

1957 - Reserve Grand Champion Fat Steers, National Western Stock Show, Denver, Colorado. Bred by Jennings Brothers Hyland Angus Ranch; fed and shown by Karl and Jack Hoffman, Ida Grove, Iowa

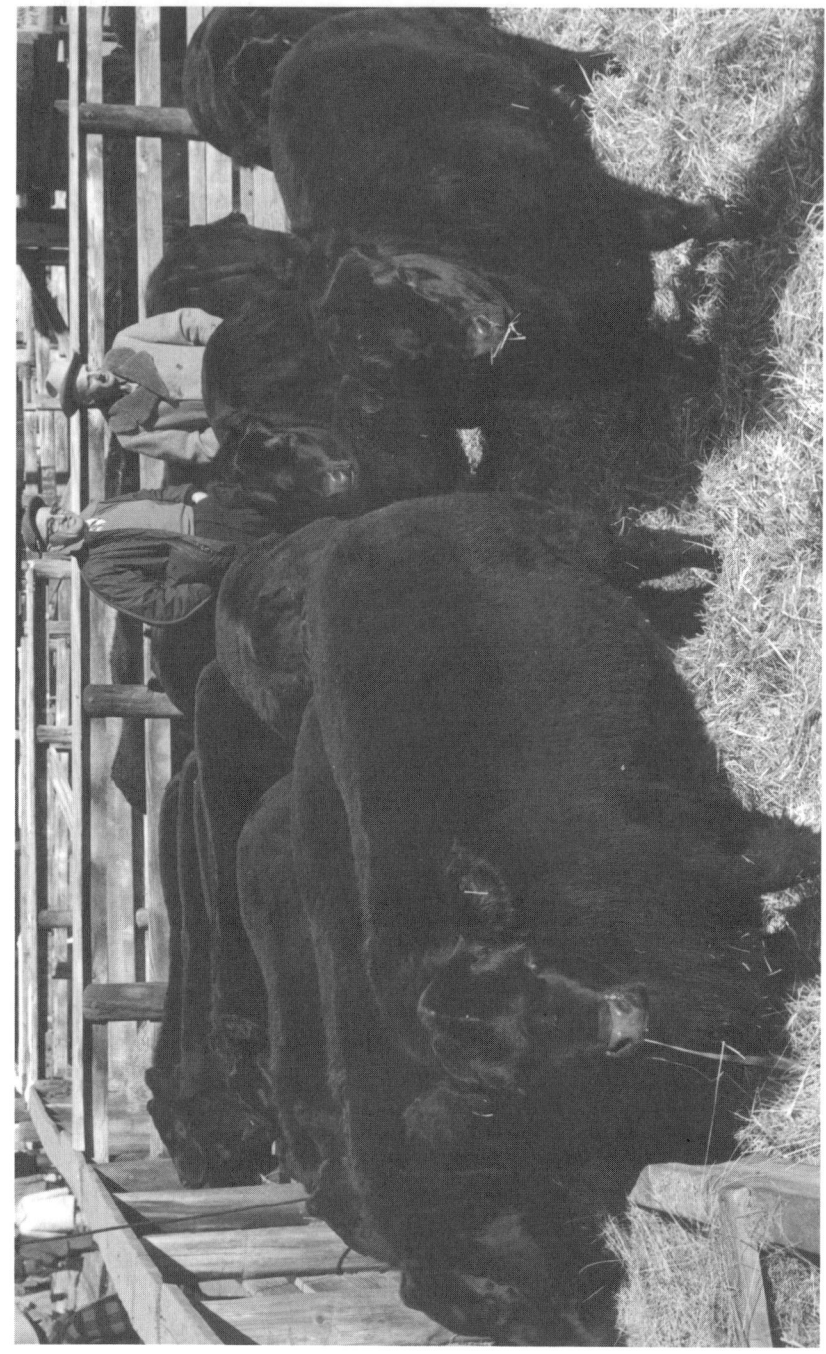

1958 - Grand Champion Fat Steers, National Western Stock Show, Denver, Colorado. Bred by Jennings Brothers Hyland Angus Ranch; fed and shown by Karl and Jack Hoffman, Karl Hoffman and Ted Jennings

1959 - Grand Champion Angus Steers, National Western Stock Show, Denver, Colorado. Bred by Jennings Brothers Hyland Angus Ranch; fed and show by Karl and Jack Hoffman, Ida Grove, Iowa. Karl Hoffman, Clayton Jennings and Jack Hoffman

1963 - Karl Hoffman with Grand Champion Angus Fat Steers at the National Western, Denver, Colorado. Bred by Jennings Brothers Hyland Angus Ranch; fed and show by Karl and Jack Hoffman, Ida Grove, Iowa

Clayton Jennings, Judge; W. J. and Bill Harrer with the Grand Champion and Reserve Champion Bulls at Helena, Montana. Clayton judged many Angus shows all over America.

Chapter 24

Showdown

In the early 1950's the Hyland Angus Ranch was running about 200 head of registered Angus cows and around 1500 commercial Angus cows. We had plans to increase the registered herd to 500 head. This expansion would enable us to more nearly meet the unusually strong demand we were experiencing for purebred Angus bulls from ranchers throughout the Dakotas, Montana, Wyoming and Nebraska.

Ralph May, one of the top young prospects in the beef cattle business, called me one day and asked if I would have a place for him on the Hyland Angus Ranch. Ralph was from Kiowa County, Oklahoma. He had received a masters degree in animal breeding in 1940 from Michigan State College, East Lansing, Michigan. Following graduation he joined the Michigan Extension Service as a livestock specialist. His work throughout Michigan brought him in close contact with a large number of Angus breeders. At the time he called me he was director of agricultural relations for Wilson and Company of Chicago. He traveled extensively throughout all the major livestock producing sections of the country. His educational and producer relations activities brought him in contact with large numbers of livestock breeders and feeders and educational agencies.

Ralph had been recommended to us by Dr. L. M. Cropsey and other Michigan State personnel. We must have talked for over an hour and I told him we were in need of a good man as we planned to increase our registered Angus herd to over 500 head of cows, but we could not pay him the kind of wages he was drawing at Wilson and Company. They were paying him well and he was moving up the ladder. He asked if he could come out and meet with me. I told him he could come any time he chose. He should let me know so I would be available at the ranch.

Clayton Jennings and Ralph May sorting cattle on the "south" Hyland Angus Ranch

About a month later he called and said he would be out in the next few days. I told him I would be around the ranch all week and I would be glad to meet with him.

Ralph was a handsome man and quite personable, but very business minded. I could see he was a very serious person. We toured the entire purebred ranch operation and saw most of the cattle. I told him of our plans to increase our registered herd over the next few years. He seemed quite pleasant in our conversation and interested in the goal we had in mind for the Hyland Angus Ranch.

That evening we sat in the sunroom of my ranch home for an extended visit about a possible job for him. We talked about wages and what I paid the other men on the ranch. I told him I doubted if I could pay him the kind of money he was worth. His plea was that he and his wife Millie had two boys, about six and eight years old, that they wanted to get out of Chicago and on a ranch. I did tell him that I wasn't beyond giving a man a good raise if he produced. Finally I said that I would start him at $100 a month more than the other ranch men were getting for being the working manager for the registered Angus cattle. He would have only me to answer to.

I was quite surprised when he said, "I'm going to work for you as soon as I can get my family here, which will be within a month." I felt sure and safe in this deal with Ralph May. He had a big job ahead of him, but I felt he could do it well.

Ralph came to work for us on March 1, 1952. We had a nice house for them to live in on the main ranch. We liked that as we wanted our managers or foremen to be on-the-job workers. I was pleased with his work and accomplishments with our registered Angus cattle. While he worked for us I sold him, on time, some registered heifers. Ralph was in charge of the artificial insemination of the cattle and it seems as though not many of his heifers were safe in calf, so I personally gave him a group of twenty heifers without charge and he seemed to be satisfied with that.

Ralph had only been with us a couple years when he told me he thought he would try another phase of life and go on his own place and I accepted that. He also decided to go into the promotion of sales and private treaty of registered Angus cattle. He had made many friends with customers of ours who came to the ranch. This put him in a position to become the sale manager of many purebred sales.

One day Calvin Gadd, a ranch neighbor of mine, and I went to one of Ralph's first sales in the south salebarn in Aberdeen, South Dakota. Calvin worked with me on many cattle deals and he could handle the details on any deals I made to get the cattle shipped to the destination and billed to whomever I might buy them for.

Cal and I pulled up in front of the salebarn in Aberdeen. The crowd was just beginning to assemble. It was about an hour before sale time. I asked Cal to go into the salebarn and get a sale catalog so we could look it over before the sale started. We started studying the sale bulls when Cal said, "Whoa, Clayton, have you seen this catalog?" I said, "Not until now, why?"

Cal showed me what was printed on the inside of the back cover. I read it. It was a short very derogative paragraph about the Hyland Angus Ranch and the Clayton Jennings' family. It was a complete shock to me and I started to burn.

I told Cal I was going to have a showdown "right now". We went into the salebarn immediately. I was ready. We met Ralph May under the bleachers just inside the door. I stopped him with no handshake only confrontation. I said, "Ralph, what were you thinking about writing this about me and my family?" I didn't give him time to answer, but I swatted him good and hard with my open right hand. Then I swatted him just as severely with my open left hand. I kept swatting him just like a machine - first with my open right hand and then my open left hand - at least half a dozen times with each hand until he went down. I never hit him one time with my fist. Then I grabbed him by the collar of his coat and asked him if he wanted more. He begged for mercy. The crowd was starting to come in so Cal held the door shut. We didn't want a big crowd around, but the fight was soon over anyway as he begged me not to slap him any more.

Cal and I went on into the salebarn and waited for the sale to begin. It was not a large sale and I bought most of the offering. Ralph was planning to buy some of the bulls for his customers, but I never let him buy an animal. With each offering I stood up and said, "Come on you s.o.b. bid!" I blew the lid off the sale.

I needed to protect my integrity and especially my family and I did!

Ralph had made a deal for a small ranch near Valentine, Nebraska, where he took his family and his forty registered cows from the Hyland Angus Ranch. While residing on the ranch near Valentine he

Ralph May, Clayton Jennings and Jack Osborne of K.T. Cattle Co. of Marysville, California. Hyland Angus Junior Bull Calves, National Western Stock Show, Denver, Colorado

acquired a job at a bank in Valentine and I understand that he advanced to president of the bank within a few years. Some time later I was going through Valentine and I stopped to inquire about him and learned of a very sad deal. Ralph was sitting on a chair at the kitchen table in his home and shot himself in the head with a pistol. He had many remarkable talents and the real reason for this act is still unknown.

Chapter 25

Walter

Walter Danekas of Raymond, South Dakota, rates well among the great humorists I have ever met. He has a dry humor and expression that you seldom find anywhere.

Our first meeting of any consequence was at the first bull sale held at the Hyland Angus Ranch in 1955, which he attended. He spread the good gospel of the Hyland Angus Ranch sale bulls and influenced many buyers to bid and buy quite a lot of bulls at this sale.

He evidently had previously taken a deep impression of me and our Angus cattle. He showed his desire to affiliate with me on many trips that we took together. He was always so happy when I asked him to go with me in my four seated chartered plane. He was constantly at my beck-and-call. He was happy to be helpful in any situation and kept my spirits up with his humorous antics.

Walter was far from a rich man and he felt I could help him move forward. He had a small herd of registered Angus cattle. They were a good basic herd and all he needed to go forward much faster was a good breeding bull. I thought to myself, "I'm going to help this young man," and I did.

Walter and I attended a Rose and McCrea sale in Missouri where Walter bought one bull and I bought several and we brought

Clayton Jennings and Mr. McCrea of Rose and McCrea, at one of the Rose and McCrea sales

them back to South Dakota together. This was the first opportunity for Walter to meet numerous influential men in the Angus business. He gained vision and inspiration from all the people attending the sale.

Everyone admired Walter for his shrewdness and fun way of life. Through our affiliation at shows and parties I kept him in the midst of every activity and he soon acquired new friends and acquaintances of real consequence.

One day when Walter was visiting the Hyland Angus Ranch he spotted a bull called Raona Bardolier 158, which was a young bull I had imported from Michigan. He liked this bull so I made a deal with him for one third interest. This one deal was the turning point in his Angus breeding program. This was a wise move for Walter. He was able to increase his income per cow by two or three times each year.

Walter says, "Clayton is my best friend. If it hadn't been for Clayton Jennings and black cattle I couldn't have accomplished what I did. I was able to raise my five children and give each of them a college education from a half section of land and forty good black cows!" Walter is very conservative, but who wouldn't have to be in a situation like that!

Following our first bull sale in 1955 we held a big party in the double garage at the Hyland Angus Ranch. We had just had a red hot sale and the whole crowd was in a glorious mood and were enjoying numerous highballs. They were throwing the stir sticks from their drinks on the floor. Walter's small young son Jim picked up a handful of the stir sticks and started selling them for a dollar a handful. He sold the first handful to J. B. McCorkle. He quickly picked up another handful and was trying to sell them when J. B. said, "Don't be a cheapskate. Buy them from the kid!"

Jim was busy all evening picking up the sticks and Myron Fuerst was heard to say, "This little guy's a promoter - he'll get someplace in life!"

When Jim was about ten, he was in 4-H and had been showing one of his dad's calves each year but he wanted a better calf to show. He called me and said that he would like to pick a show calf out of the Hyland Angus herd. I told him to come down and he could select any calf from a pen of about a hundred. I had the calves penned when Walter and Jim arrived. It was quite confusing for Jim as they were all so uniform and alike. He picked out the one he thought was a good show prospect. Then we went down town in Miller for something to eat.

Jim had the cash in his pocket to pay for the calf. He thought he could buy it for $100. Finally he said, "Mr. Jennings, how much do you want for the calf?"

I didn't answer right away. I wanted Jim to think this was a big decision for me. Finally I said, "Old timer, this one's on me! It's a gift from the Hyland Angus Ranch!"

Walter Danekas and Clayton Jennings - 1995 - one of Walter's Studebakers in the background

The calf developed well and showed well and stood second in his class at the South Dakota State Fair. Jim was very proud of his achievement.

Walter is retired now. He leases out his land to a neighbor on a share basis. He now refurbishes ancient Studebaker cars. This hobby has been most pleasant and rewarding for him in his retirement.

Walter Danekas and I became good friends on our first meeting and today our friendship is more cherished than ever. His is a great story from the grassroots of the prairie of South Dakota.

Chapter 26

J. C. Penney

In 1954 the Hyland Angus Ranch had an outstanding Angus steer named Blackjack. We had raised this steer and we felt he was the greatest. We entered him in several shows around the country and he had been named Grand Champion of every show.

We decided to enter him in the Chicago International, which was the most prestigious show at that time. Anyone who thought they had a good show animal could enter it in that show and they would know just how good it was. It was just like shooting at the moon!

The livestock barn in Chicago was full of outstanding steers of all breeds and all ages. To win a championship the steer had to be completely ready at the time he was shown. Argyl Conner, our herdsman, was a great showman and he would be showing Blackjack. They made a great team. Blackjack won each class division and was ready for the championship division.

In the championship division we found that we would be showing against an Angus steer raised at Penney and James Angus Farm of Hamilton, Missouri, one of the most highly reputable Angus

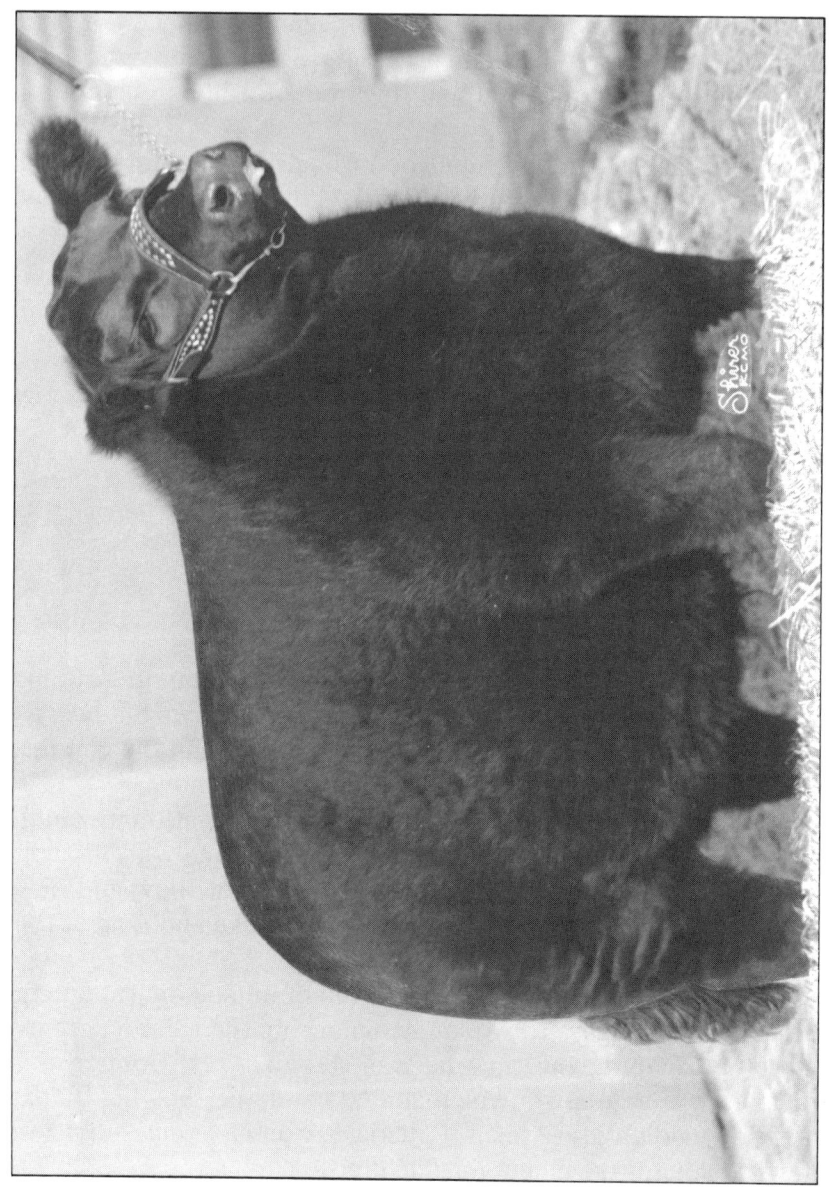

Hyland Blackjack - Reserve Grand Champion at the Chicago International, Chicago, Illinois

The steer that beat us! Raised by Penney and James Angus Farms and shown by a 4-H girl

breeding establishment in the business. Their steer was shown by a 4-H girl. She was an excellent showman and was odds on favorite to most of the crowd.

We had a lot of pullers for our steer Blackjack, too, and we were quite confident that we could beat the Penney and James steer. Without question the judge showed a lot of time and attention to both steers and took more time than with the bigger classes all together.

There was unusual suspense with the entire crowd waiting to see which steer would be Grand Champion. Suddenly the judge slapped the rump of the Penney and James bred steer shown by the 4-H girl as Grand Champion of the show and making Blackjack Reserve Grand Champion.

We believed in our steer and we still did. He went on to become Champion Angus Steer and Reserve Grand Champion Steer of All Breeds at the 1955 National Western Stock Show in Denver.

The evening after the show in Chicago there was an Angus banquet at the Stockyards Inn for the annual recognition of the champions. About 20 minutes before the banquet as I was mingling with the crowd, a man in a tuxedo came up to me and asked that I follow him as he had a seat reserved for me. The banquet room was large. It surely would hold a thousand or more and was quite an elegant affair. The man in the tuxedo showed me to my seat and next to me was seated J. C. Penney and next to him was the 4-H girl who showed the winning steer. I was pleasantly shocked to be able to sit and visit with J. C. Penney. I immediately recognized him as a very distinguished gentleman and I felt highly honored. During our conversation he invited me to his production sale at Hamilton, Missouri, the home of Penney and James Angus Farm.

I attended several of the production sales in Hamilton and always enjoyed the events very much. In fact I looked forward to them, as it was always worthwhile talking to J. C. Penney. In rating of the distinguished gentlemen I have met, he would be among the top of my list.

J. C. Penney - 1962

Clayton Jennings contemplating his next purchase at a Penney and James Sale, Hamilton, Missouri

Chapter 27

Wilbur's Feed and Seed Store

In August 1950 Charlie Wilbur, a former shop teacher in the Miller school system, opened Wilbur's Feed and Seed Store. As the name implies it was a retail feed, seed and farm supply store.

The Hyland Angus Ranch started doing business with him right away. It was a pleasure to work with him as he had good advice to give in regard to our seed program. We bought mostly seed from

Clayton Jennings and Charlie Wilbur - 1994

him to put in crops and hay and to seed some farm land to bromegrass, crested wheatgrass and alfalfa.

In May 1955 to help Charlie out and make his feed store better known in the area, Ted furnished a 400 pound Angus calf, from the Hyland Angus Ranch, to Charlie for a feed demonstration. The steer was named Little Black Joe. They fed him all summer in the back room of the store. He gained three pounds a day. Charlie sent out bulletins every two weeks, which created a lot of interest. People stopped by every day to see the steer.

In October 1955 Charlie held a feeder meeting and beef barbecue. It was a glorious affair with eight hundred people attending. They enjoyed a menu of baked beans, buns and Little Black Joe.

Charlie became one of the biggest successes in this part of the country - going from a shop teacher to a seed dealer - nationally recognized and patronized.

Charlie Wilbur is one of the great contributors to the welfare of South Dakota. He is highly respected for his knowledge and what he did for Miller and the surrounding area.

****

July 4, 1995

CLAYTON AND TED JENNINGS
IN A CLASS BY THEMSELVES

In 1950 as a fledgling businessman fresh out of teaching school in Miller, any sale that I made, large or small, contributed to my surviving the transition. One day in early September, when the sales were small and when the survival issue was still very much in doubt, Clayton met me in front of the First National Bank in Miller and asked me if I would provide him with enough bromegrass seed for the fall planting of more than a section of ground. And if so would I deliver it? He wanted no discount. Free delivery to their ranches would suffice. The profit on the sale was $540.00. I had just quit teaching at a salary of less than $10.00 per day. You can imagine my gratitude, as today's saying goes, "He made my day!" But in this stance he made my day alright; clear into next year and beyond. One thing is for sure, as of that moment all my inner doubts of my success in the feed and seed business vanished right there with that conversation with Clayton. What he asked me to do any of half a dozen dealers would have done, but he knew that I might need a boost and he was giving me one. I have never forgotten it, nor what it did for me.

As our business dealings grew, so did our friendship. By nature the Jennings were friendly, always optimistic, generous to a fault and, in general, fun to be around.

They were very prosperous not only because of their superior knowledge of cattle, but also of ranching, marketing and marketing trends. But there was another factor involved which was more important than all of the rest and which they had an abundance. That was integrity. Integrity in all forms of business dealings was their code. They learned this from their father and it was their way of doing business right from the start.

Times have changed and with it went their kind of men and that manner of doing business. People felt that Clayton's or Ted's word or a handshake over a deal was better than any contract any man could write, so none was written nor any detail ever forgotten. Many, many times I've heard that statement from ranchers about the Jennings Brothers and the value of their word. They spoke with pride, too, of some past personal experiences with Clayton and Ted, further verifying their own belief in them. A banker friend enjoyed saying that the total belief by the cattle industry, in the integrity of the Jennings Brothers, was unbelievable.

These stories of their business practices were to become a tremendous influence for good in all business in our area and for miles around.

In closing I remember this conversation with Clayton. He once said to me, "It isn't easy to be in business and make friends and money both. You have to work at it constantly or you might lose the friend and maybe the sale too. If you find the load too heavy, Charlie, concentrate more on making and keeping friends and I have found that the money follows!"

Clayton and Ted, I thank you both. It has been a pleasure.
s/s C. J. Wilbur

Chapter 28

Junior Suhn - Commercial Ranch Foreman

When Ted and I bought the Sandkamp place we were just beginning to put the Hyland Ranch together. The Ernest Suhn, Jr. family was working on the place at the time. He seemed to be an eager, willing young man, so we hired him to stay with the ranch and work for us. We soon made him foreman of the commercial cattle division, a position that he held until his untimely early death.

As the Hyland Angus Ranch grew Junior and Loretta and their five children grew with us. He had the knack of knowing every cow in the herd and was able to get them bred and calved out better than anyone. Loretta was an excellent cook and homemaker. She easily handled all the extra cooking, housekeeping and the book work associated with the commercial ranch. They were a family of people that really worked great with the cattle and the ranch. We were lucky and privileged to have the Suhn family work for the Hyland Angus Ranch.

OUR HOME - THE HYLAND ANGUS RANCH

When Ted and Clayton Jennings were putting the Hyland Angus Ranch together, we were living on the Otto Sandkamp place. Ted and Clayton bought this land in 1946 and we stayed on to work for them. I remember our first wages were $75.00 a month.

During the winters we were snowbound a lot. The roads were not graded at that time so we were snowed in or mudded in most of the time. During the winter of 1948 after we had been unable to get to town for several weeks, we were out of meat. We contacted Clayton and he picked up some meat for us at the locker plant in Ree Heights, South Dakota. The only way for him to get to our ranch was by horseback. He rode a horse through the deep snow the three miles from Highway 14 to our

Junior Suhn with young sons, Dale, Vern and Jerry heat detecting on the Hyland Angus Ranch

place. He was a beautiful sight to see. Clayton stayed for dinner, we were having beef stew (the last of our meat) and dumplings.

Ted and Clayton bought the Buck Steers ranch and it became our home from 1950 until the end of our stay with the Hyland Angus Ranch. This was the headquarters for the commercial division and Junior became the commercial division foreman. What a change - electricity, running water, and two bathrooms where the boys (Jerry and Vern) had a ball flushing the stool and watching the water run.

Artificial insemination was a major part of the breeding program at the Hyland Angus Ranch. While other ranches were turning out bulls in the spring of the year, we spent countless hours in the saddle detecting and bringing "heats" into the corrals for such skilled technicians as Rand and Phil VanDervoort. They were driven in a slow manner into the corrals by riders on horseback. It is very important to have patience and not excite the cows or heifers. Beginning in June all five of the Suhn children did a great lot of heat detecting - day after day - for about 30 days, depending on how many cows are settled during a heat period. It was an all day job, every day, checking for heats at daylight, then during the middle part of the day and again in late evening before dark.

As the Hyland Angus Ranch was one of the first commercial operations to use AI on a large scale we witnessed many changes from the use of fresh semen, to frozen semen in glass ampules, to the frozen semen in straws. Although it required more time and extra labor, it afforded us the opportunity to use the best genetics available. Moreover the large numbers of half-sisters added greatly to the uniformity and consistency in the commercial herd. We were able to evaluate the genetics of the new-era Angus bulls.

We always had hired hands staying in the bunkhouse on our ranch. In the summer it was the haying crew, which was made up of many college kids. It was constant cooking, doing the dishes, cleaning and keeping records. Sometimes we would liven it up a bit. On April Fool's Day we would put a filter disk in their pancake or a string in the coconut cream pie.

As we reflect on our life on the Hyland Angus Ranch, we are thankful for the opportunities and experiences that it provided - opportunities and experiences that most people do not have in a lifetime. Some seemed of no consequence at the time, but have proved invaluable in later life.

Growing up and with the Hyland Angus Ranch and knowing Ted and Clayton Jennings is an experience everyone should have. And being a part of this great ranch is something that we would not trade for anything in the world!

Clayton and Ted Jennings will probably never be fully appreciated for what they did for the beef industry and for the people in the Highmore and Miller areas. They were always willing to help people out in hard times and provide support to keep them going. They were a definite boost to the economy of the area, always buying feed and cattle, having cattle fed, renting, and hiring people in the area. They were "economic development" for agriculture in a large area of South Dakota.

/s/ Mrs. Ernest (Loretta) Suhn, Jr.
Barbara, Jerry, Vern, Dale and Kathleen

I have become better acquainted with Clayton after LeAnn and I moved onto his old ranch headquarters in 1978. Clayton would come and visit and recall different things that had happened in the past. We trade a few cattle and he has been very supportive of our first bull sales held at the ranch.

I am very honored to have had the opportunity to know Clayton Jennings and I believe him to be a good friend. There are few people of his stature.

/s/ Dale Suhn

(Dale Suhn and his family live on my old ranch. He is the resident manager of the Eagle Pass Ranch.)

Clayton Jennings and Junior Suhn sorting cattle on the commercial headquarters - 1962. Junior was the foreman of the commercial cattle. He had a knack of knowing every cow in the herd. He always was able to get them bred and calved out as good as any man.

Jerry, Dale, Loretta, Barbara Law, Kathleen Marsden and Vern Suhn - 1990

Chapter 29

I'll Do the Best I Can

The following story was written by Harold, Phyllis, Larry and David Parlin, loyal employees of the Hyland Angus Ranch for many years. The whole family was an important key to the success of the Hyland Angus Ranch.

When I first met Harold in 1956 he was working for a local contractor on the construction of the sale barn at our ranch headquarters. I kept watching him every day working on the roof of the barn. I couldn't believe that anyone could work so steady and precise and with so much dedication day in and day out. As I watched I decided I had to hire this guy as I believed he would make a wonderful addition to our ranch crew. And I was right, as he and his family were among the greatest ever to work for the Hyland Angus Ranch.

I'LL DO THE BEST I CAN

Would you hire a man, his wife and two little boys, 11 and 8, knowing they seemed to have the reputation of jumping from one job to another? This is what Harold Parlin, his wife Phyllis and sons Larry and David seemed to be doing from 1945 to 1956. They were a hard working family and needed "just a little luck". Luck came their way in March 1956 along with employment that lasted over 21 years on the same place. Thanks to Clayton Jennings and the Hyland Angus Ranch. Clayton's faith and trust will never be forgotten nor will being a man of his word as he has proven over and over.

Explaining our reputation of one job to another seems almost impossible now. We wonder how our family of four got by. One job we worked spring to fall - relieved of our duties during the winter - $150 per month with no benefits. Another lasted three years - share basis not to exceed $150 per month. We received $75 per month with no benefits whatsoever. One story is hard to believe. We gathered thirty dozen eggs a week,

The Hyland Angus Ranch sale barn with the white letters on the roof - layed by Harold Parlin in 1955

cleaned and had them ready for market, but we had to buy eggs for our own use. None of the homes we lived in were modern, meaning no lights, water or bath. Heat was provided by oil burners or by burning corn cobs in a Round Oak cookstove, which was also used for cooking.

In 1953 Harold hired out as a carpenter and the family lived in Highmore. We did have lights but no other conveniences. In 1954 and 1955 Harold helped build the Jennings Brothers sale barn at the Hyland Angus Ranch headquarters. He helped lay the white letters HYLAND ANGUS RANCH on the roof of the sale barn. Many pilots have landed their planes in the alfalfa field, thanks to the lettering on the roof of the barn. Harold is proud to this day that he had a part in this inlaid lettering.

After working all day on the sale barn, Harold would help out some evenings in Dale's Tavern in Highmore. One March evening in 1956 a good looking cowboy with a black hat came in and sat up to the bar. He introduced himself and said he had been watching Harold work on the salebarn.

"How would you like to work for me? Looks like your a hellava worker!" he said.

"You mean on the ranch with your black cattle?" Harold beamed. His only thought was - I was never meant to be a carpenter. Harold couldn't believe he had just met Clayton Jennings "The master of masters" whom everyone seemed to know. Luck was finally coming our way.

Several days later we went out to the ranch with Clayton. We plowed through drifted snow on the road at least four or five feet deep all the way. He showed us the home we'd be living in if we took the job. It was next to the beautiful sale barn with the white letters. What a beautiful home - we couldn't believe our eyes! AND wouldn't you know, it even had electric lights, water really coming from the faucets, a bathroom (not an outhouse) and a gorgeous kitchen with cupboards galore! The boys' room upstairs was wallpapered with cowboys and Indians. Just wait until they see this. They won't believe their eyes!

NOW it was time to get down to brass tacks. "What does your deal have to offer, Mr. Jennings?" Harold hurriedly asked.

Clayton said with a smile, "Going wages, all the meat you can eat (beef, pork and chickens), heat, milk and eggs. Your

May 1958 - Kids on the Ranch - Cheryl and Mike Hahn on Blacky, Larry Parlin, Gloria Jennings, Charlie Jennings and David Parlin on Spot

wife may have to cook for some hired hands but we'll pay her $1.00 per meal." Above everything else we would have our first modern home! Clayton looked at Harold and asked, "What's your decision?" Tears came, a lump formed in Harold's throat, they shook hands and the deal was on. Harold replied, "I'LL DO THE VERY BEST I CAN!"

Our new boss looked at us and we knew he had something more on his mind. He said, "I'll have to tell you kids as I've told all my hired hands. Use all you want of everything and enjoy all the things I offer but the waste of any of these privileges I will not tolerate!"

As new employees we wasted no time in moving to the Hyland Angus Ranch. We were concerned, however, because Clayton was going through a divorce. We handled the situation with very few problems although it was hard on the children.

Sept. 1960 - Charlie Jennings, Larry Parlin, Jim Leachman, David Parlin and their 4-H show calves

Harold's respect for Clayton to this very day is of the highest regard. Through him he learned the Angus business with honesty, integrity, compassion and the love for black cattle. He learned good cows from bad cows, good productive bulls from the ordinary. Clayton taught him that those little black babies needed extra TLC and Harold always saw that they got it.

There were cattle records and bookkeeping to be done so an office was set up in their home. This was all new to Phyllis but she was willing to give it a try. Clayton was a super teacher and taught her the registration and record business. She thanks him sincerely and credits him with the fact that she kept cattle records for 35 years!

Larry and David learned how to select their own 4-H calves, break them to lead and show them in the ring. Clayton had them earn their calves. They kept track of the feed and other expenses. After the 4-H Club calf sale they would reimburse him. At times the boys thought they were mistreated, especially at the State Fair. After showing their animals most kids would go to the carnival and the parents would take care of their calves. But Clayton and his showman saw to it that the boys washed their calves and bedded them down before any pleasure. Usually the carnival rides were over by the time they got done.

The Parlin boys will tell you to this day they have Clayton high on a pedestal and he is a man they shall never forget. He did so much for them as little boys and young men. When they graduated from high school his graduation gift to them was a trip to Huron, South Dakota, where he bought each of them a suit from Dave Johnson at Osborn's. This was Clayton Jennings, the man with a heart of gold.

Our first vacation was a cattle show at Great Falls, Montana. Just before leaving Clayton dipped into his pocket and gave the boys each a $20 bill to spend as they wished. Even though these little boys are now 49 and 46 they still pay tribute to a great man with love and respect.

We got our first new car in 1959 thanks to Clayton Jennings. We had a 1949 Plymouth but he wanted us to have a better car. One day he cornered us and a car discussion was held. After concentration and adjusting his black hat. He said, "I'll tell you kids what I'll do. I"ll give you the price of a bull or $700 as a

April 1995 - Harold and Phyllis Parlin's 50th Wedding Anniversary. Their son's David and Larry toasting them

down payment and you can buy a different car." Not long after that we went to Miller, South Dakota, and purchased a 1959 Chevrolet. This man's goodness was never ending. The 1949 Plymouth was kept in good use for heat detecting cows and for pleasure. Larry cut the top off and we used it on the ranch and all the kids had hours of enjoyment.

Our little white house by the sale barn was Grand Central Station for Rand VanDerVoort, Phil Hazzard, Jim Drayson and many other artificial inseminators. Their families came and stayed in our basement. Many of them ate with us. Artificial insemination was a fairly new process back then. We remember Rand gathering fresh eggs and mixing the drawn semen in our kitchen. We met many people through the inseminators.

We still keep in touch with Clayton and his wife Carol. We've known Carol for many years and she is a super fine person. This is a team that would be judged " top class" placed in any ring on the face of the earth.

The PARLINS love you Clayton. We started with just a little bit of luck - but that luck grew thanks to you! Your faith and belief in us is a cherished memory and will never be forgotten. Clayton, you knew I'd keep my promise and write this story because I've always maintained, "I'LL DO THE BEST I CAN"!

Chapter 30

The Late 40's and 50's With Doc Cropsey

It was 1949, I was talking to my good friend, Ray Smith, of Raona Farms and he mentioned a young veterinarian by the name of Dr. L. M. Cropsey who was working with many purebred Angus breeders to increase the efficiency of their herds.

At the time Hyland Angus had acquired a bull by the name of Hyland Marshall. He was considered a most outstanding Angus bull but had a low fertility rate. With Ray Smith's assistance, I contacted Dr. Cropsey and asked him to make a trip to the Hyland Angus Ranch and stay in my home.

Ted and I and Ralph May, my purebred manager, thought Dr. Cropsey's recommendations for Hyland Marshall were worth trying. To our pleasant surprise after Cropsey's prescribed treatment his fertility rate did improve.

From this initial visit of Dr. Cropsey's in the late 1940's to this time, which is nearly 50 years, Doc and I have had one of the best friendships. We had mutual confidence and complete trust of each others verbal commitments to follow through on our promises. We have shared each others difficult problems, both business and personal, through all these 50 years. Our word for each other was 100%.

In the early 1950's Dr. Cropsey was convinced by Dr. Armond Hammer to move East and join his Shadow Isle staff at Red Bank, N.J. I went to Red Bank and bought a truckload of bulls from Dr. Cropsey. I attended several of their sales where registered Angus females bred artificially to their famous herd sire, Prince Eric, were selling for an average of $5000.00 in the early 50's.

In 1955 I called Dr. Cropsey to Hyland as Ted and I found that our calf crop was shrinking and we had too many open cows. Again Cropsey had the correct diagnosis of our problem which was trichomonosis in some of our older bulls. Trichomonosis causes early abortion in cows. His recommendations were severe. He told us to dispose of all the older infected bulls and any cows that were not safe in calf after 4 months. However, Cropsey said we could salvage the open cows after a complete 90 day breeding rest by using artificial insemination. The cows gain an immunity, for life, after this 90 day rest. We could use fresh semen from our best "trich" free bulls. The semen could be extended with an egg yolk and sodium citrate solution and be used over a 3 or 4 day period to breed 100 cows. (Frozen semen was not available in the 50's.)

Ted and I did not know much about artificial insemination (AI), but after much consideration we decided to give it a try and we became the first large herd to pioneer this program. Dr. Cropsey promised us a well-qualified inseminator. He recommended Rand

L. M. "Doc" Cropsey, G. J. Six, Clayton Jennings and Dale Christensen in Denver - 1995

VanDervoort, who had been associated with him at Curtiss Candy Farms in Illinois and at Shadow Isle Farms in New Jersey.

Cropsey and VanDervoort arrived at the ranch to start our first AI. Ted and I had to rely on their judgment and experience to make AI successful. Our ranch hands had to learn to observe the cows in early "heat" and carefully and quietly bring them into the breeding corrals. The men carried a note book to keep each cow's record and time of observation so each one could be inseminated at the optimum time of conception, which was 12 to 24 hours after the first observation of "heat". We were fortunate to have good cow men who carried out all the details prescribed by Cropsey and VanDervoort which made our first AI pay off and of course, cleaned up our herd from Trichomonosis, which we never had again in our herd.

Our first calves were very uniform and like "peas in a pod". Karl and Jack Hoffman of Ida Grove, Iowa, were so impressed with our AI calves that they purchased them every year to feed and show at all the major shows, always winning Grand Champion with their carload lots of steers.

It was most obvious to Ted and me that we keep breeding AI as it was practical and profitable with our large herd. Our reputation for uniform high-quality Angus cattle, both commercial and registered, grew tremendously in the late 50's. Thanks to Cropsey and VanDervoort and their good AI program.

Rand VanDervoort returned every summer to take charge of the artificial insemination. We used the AI program as long as we had cattle. With Rand's success in our herd he also was able to make many other area ranchers AI successful.

According to Doc Cropsey, the Hyland Angus Ranch was the largest and most successful Angus AI program in North America.

Chapter 31

Rand VanDervoort and Artificial Insemination

by Phil VanDervoort

Rand VanDervoort came to work for Hyland Angus Ranch in 1954 and continued to head up the insemination program here until the late 1970's. The Hyland Angus Ranch AI program proved to be the largest and longest continuous running beef A. I. program until the dispersal of the herds in the mid 1980's. Over a 31 year period, more than 139,540 head were artificially inseminated.

Rand worked for Curtiss Candy Company Farms, Cary, Illinois, in the mid 1940's. While there he was in charge of all records for their large herds of registered Holsteins, Brown Swiss, Ayrshires and Guernseys. This in itself was more than a full time occupation. However, he also developed a record and identification system of ear notching for the large purebred hog operation that Curtiss Candy had at the time. Curtiss operated at least four hog herds of 500 head each of four different breeds. It was at this time that Dr. L. M. "Mac" Cropsey, the Curtiss resident veterinarian taught Rand how to AI the large dairy herd. Rand became the first AI technician for Curtiss Candy Company Farms. This company became Curtiss Breeding Service and was the largest AI company for many years.

In 1949 Rand moved from Curtiss over to the Northern Illinois Breeding Co-op and bred in the Elgin, Illinois, area for a time. In 1950 Rand started AIing beef herds in conjunction with Dr. Cropsey. About this time, Rand accepted a job of being in charge of all AI for Shadow Isle Farms of Red Bank and Colt's Neck, New Jersey. This operation was owned by Dr. Armond Hammer and fast became one of the most outstanding purebred Angus herds in the world. While here, Rand collected the semen from the herd sires and bred the cows with fresh fluid semen.

Rand moved his family from New Jersey to Broken Bow, Nebraska, in 1953 as he felt that beef AI would be natural and rela-

Rand VanDervoort — 1966

tively easy to promote in ranching country. Rand was ahead of his time and it was a really hard sell to get ranchers to try something so new and unknown. However, there was a handful (small) of progressive minded ranchers who could realize the benefits of AI. Among these were Wilbur Drybread of Valentine, the Keller Brothers of Broken Bow and Purdum and the Jennings Brothers up in South Dakota. In 1954 Rand spent his first of many summers in the Highmore, South Dakota area.

Starting from scratch, Clayton and Ted Jennings were able to visualize the tremendous benefits of AI in their herds and other herds. They were most receptive to Rand's suggestions for achieving the best results possible. Facilities were improved upon or built from scratch. Cowboys were instructed on heat detection and timing and the different ranch unit managers were pumped up by the Jennings to achieve their goals. Some of the key men who made the program work in those days were Junior Suhn, Harold Parlin, Jim Blair, and Jimmy Krick just to name a few.

The Hyland Angus purebred operations had raised and acquired some of the top Angus sires of the time. Each day Rand would collect the semen from certain bulls and breed the cows with fresh fluid semen. Many times there were more cows to breed than there was semen available and Rand and Harold Parlin would work the Hyland bulls long and hard to get enough semen to do the job that day. At this time, many of the cows were inseminated twice in 24 hours to insure the best conception rates possible. Once frozen semen was perfected, it made life easier for both Rand and the bulls. In 1958 Hyland Angus achieved a 71% calf out conception on over 1000 head of cows inseminated.

As Rand proved that range country AI would work, the Jennings started AIing their commercial herds. Soon Clayton had the neighbors also using AI. Clayton and Ted started buying their neighbors calves and paying high prices. This started a landslide and probably more beef cows were AI'd in Hyde, Hand and Faulk counties in South Dakota during the early and mid 1960's than anywhere else in the world. Clayton and Ted would tell Rand to go visit a certain rancher and when Rand left he had another 200 or 300 head to AI. This explosion of AI created a need for additional technicians and Rand found and used good ones. Some of these technicians that ran the country roads around Highmore, Ree Heights and Miller were Bill and Chet Farrell, Max Beyeler, Bob

1950's - Rand VanDervoort doing his AI work out of the back of his station wagon

Behrens, Dick Myers, Jack Trinkle, Ralph Williams, Vern Davis and Jim Drayson.

As more herds began to AI Rand put together "pools" of herds to make AI more economical for the ranchers. "Pooling" allowed for better semen prices and better technicians fees. Each technician had a certain set of ranches where he did the work and he would arrive there at a designated time both morning and evening. Using the time table, the technician would work five to seven locations twice a day. Generally at the end of four weeks, the technician had inseminated 1000 to 2000 head. Most programs went for at least 28 days and many for 30 days. This time frame allowed Rand to calculate a pregnancy rate and he was very seldom off on his figures. Many times his record work and calculation would be within a 1 or 2% of the AI calf out. The Jennings would purchase many of these calves and send them all over the U. S. on orders from buyers looking for uniform high quality replacement females. About this time, Hyland Angus steers were winning the Carload Lots at the Chicago International and the National Western in Denver. Hyland Angus was well known from coast to coast as the place to go for load after load of half sister replacements or for uniform high quality steers to feed.

Rand was meticulous in his record keeping and he demanded the same from his technicians. Rand devised a record system with a series of checks and balances and it was easy to keep track of large numbers and never miss a cow. His records were invaluable for both the purebred and commercial operations.

South Dakota summers can be long and hot and the days for everyone doing AI programs would really get long after the first 21 days of the season. Pranks and jokes became a part of the wind down every year. About every year, Junior Suhn would prime Rand for one of his favorite stunts. Junior would let Rand know he had 30 to 40 head to breed in the afternoon. About the time Rand would arrive and drive through the gates, here would come all the cows on a dead run for the gate. Rand would frantically try to stop them and not get the job done. If you knew Rand, you would know that this was real panic for him. For Junior and his cowboys, it was great sport to see Rand trying to stop 40 head of cows that weren't in heat anyway, going out the gate. Junior pulled this stunt on Rand several times and it always worked like a charm.

Rand's determination to make beef AI work on a practical basis moved the Hyland Angus Ranch to the forefront of providing large numbers of half brother bulls and half sister heifers. At one time, Hyland had herds of 500 to over 1000 head that were all half sisters. The extensive use of AI allowed Ted and Clayton to develop what was probably the most uniform set of Angus cows that the industry has ever seen.

Chapter 32

From Summer Hay Crew to AI Technician

by Phil VanDervoort

I believe I was six years old when my dad, Rand, started his artificial insemination work. I literally grew up with the AI industry but didn't have much interest in it until I started working on ranches and around cattle. I first went to work for Hyland Angus Ranch in 1957 and basically did work for them every year until the final herds were dispersed. In 1957 I went to work for Clayton and stayed with Harold and Phyllis Parlin on the main ranch. I was hired, along with 20 or 30 other men to help put up the thousands of acres of hay and silage that the ranch used.

The summer crews for Hyland Angus came from all over the country, Iowa, Illinois, Michigan, the Dakotas and as far away as New York. One summer I bunked with Jim Leachman at the bull ranch which was run by Bud and Elinor Hahn. Jim and I stayed there all summer and left in the fall for college.

The hay crew stacked tens of thousands of small round bales every year. There were about 1500 bales in each stack and many stacks were placed so silage could be piled between them. On a good day the crew could haul in excess of 3000 bales from the field to the stack yards. One year the crew stacked bales well into the fall, October I believe. Using International "M's" and "H's" with stackers on them, bales were loaded on trucks in the fields and then hauled to the yards and restacked. I remember that those little round bales shed twine something terrible and everyone kept sharp sickle sections welded to their bale hooks to cut the strings. A lot of loose hay was also put up and we all served time on the stack straightening the hay that was pushed off on the stack with the stacker. In later years they didn't put anyone up on the stack and it was much easier work. With the hay crews as big as they were, there were many a Monday morning when only part of the crew worked while the rest recovered from too many dances and too much beer. The hay crews on the "north ranch" were run by Jim Blair and Bob Fratzke. They taught a lot of young guys how to put hay up right.

When the weather wouldn't allow haying, the crews picked rock, which grow in the hay and crop fields in central South Dakota. The rocks were piled in big piles in the fields and during the 60's when the Big Bend Dam was being built, the rocks were hauled to the dam for rip-rap. Another chore was to paint the fences at Hyland Angus, black on the posts and white on the boards. The black was a heavy tar mixture and a real mess if you weren't careful. One time, Dick Ross, I believe he was a nephew of Clayton's, decided to bury some of the tar, which he did, but I believe that Junior Suhn, the manager at the time, found out about the deal and he found more tar so the boys could "keep at it until your done". No more tar was buried after that.

Clayton had a favorite saying that he always told everyone building fences and buildings for him, "If you're going to build fences or corrals, build them hell for stout." All of Hyland's facilities were "Hell for Stout" and there was never any doubt about that.

In the fall of 1961 I was staying in the bunkhouse at Junior Suhn's and going over to help Jim Blair feed 1000 or more heifer calves every day. Jim fed with a team in those days. We'd load silage and dehydrated pellets on a flat bed, haul this to the pens, and scoop it off into feed bunks. I thought there surely must be an easier way to make a living than putting up hay all day. I mentioned to Jim one day that it sure looked like being an AI technician was the job to have. You worked early in the morning when it was cool, did your bookwork in the middle of the day when it was hot and then bred cows again in the evening when it was cool. Jim urged me to get lined up for AI school and that's what I eventually did in the fall of 1962. I went to Illinois to AI school. I worked for the old Northern Illinois Breeding Co-op breeding dairy cows before coming back west to AI beef cows which I still do today.

Before Rand would let me breed any cattle for the Jennings', he had to be sure I could get the job done right. I was used as a follow-up technician for the repeat work for a few years. One of the prerequisites for a technician at Hyland Angus was that he be able to inseminate 40 head per hour. The cowboys pushed the cow up the chute and the inseminator only had to load his pipette, breed the cow, keep the record of the cow's ID and the bull used and the collection code of the semen used!

In the early days of artificial insemination, fluid (fresh) semen was used. Every other day for several summers, someone would drive to the airport at Pierre and pick up fresh semen flown in from International Beef Breeders in Denver.

There are always a few events that stay in your memory and there are several that occurred when breeding at Hyland Angus. Junior Suhn was a serious manager and everyone took him that way, including his family. For several summers, Vern Suhn(Junior's son) and John Blair detected on the replacement heifers. One day we had a good run of 30 or more to breed. The chute would hold 10 or 11 heifers behind the technician. We were down to the last chute full and the men told me they had 12 left to do. I pulled 12 ampules of semen and bred 11 head and was told "That's all." I questioned the count and we checked the heifers that were bred and we were short one. Vern looked down the chute and there was our shortage, over on her back and as dead as a wedge. The heifer had been the last one in the chute. She reared up and was pushed over backwards and in the solid chute no one saw her until it was too late. I guess I have never seen anyone get so serious as Vern did. He knew he was in deep water with his dad on this deal. So he got the farmhand and hung the heifer up, gutted her and took her to the locker plant. I doubt to this day that Vern ever packs a chute full when working cattle.

At the Hyland ranches we always had a kid or two around to keep things lively as they always came around when the "breeder" got there. One little guy in particular, probably 5 or 6 years old, was really taken with the AI deal. His dad told us he caught him trying to inseminate a chicken with one of the used pipettes out of the trash. He also tried to inseminate a bucket calf and broke the rod off in the calf and his dad had to retrieve the broken rod from the calf. Naturally we got to teasing him about breeding chickens and one thing led to another. He was full of questions about AI breeding and the birds and bees in general. I had a couple old amps rolling around in my breeding kit and of course he spotted these right away. He just had to have them. We told him he could have them and a clean pipette but he would have to suck the semen up into the pipette before he could use it. Just as we figured, he ended up with a mouth full of semen which cracked everyone up but him. Now he was in trouble as he thought he was going to be pregnant. He was pretty worried when he left the corrals. He must have carried the worry to the house as the next day his dad came out and told us maybe we should back off the kidding for a while. I guess that we did, for a day or so anyway.

Along the side of a large barn on one of the ranches were sorting pens that led to the chute. Any rain would turn this into a real mudhole and then the cattle were sometimes hard to work in this area. One day in this muddy condition the heifers would not cooperate and feed into the chute. The hand who was working the cattle was using a baseball bat for a sorting stick. About the third time the heifers broke back on him he took a swing with his sorting bat and five minutes later Hyland Angus had another beef hung from the stacker. Needless to say, no more baseball bats were used for sorting sticks.

Lowell Krog lived on the "south end" of Hyland Angus for years and usually had 500 to 600 head of cattle to take care of. Krog was a jumpy kind of guy and was always good for a few laughs every season. Sometimes during the real hot weather, the technician would take a cooler of beer and pop to the riders and everyone would hustle to get done so they could have a beer break. Terry Krick had caught a bull snake (a harmless snake) about five feet long and we knew Krog was spooked by snakes. That day I had an empty cooler, so in the snake went. I was driving a small car at the time and the cooler sat on the floor on the passenger side. When we got done breeding at Krog's I mentioned I had my cooler in the front seat. Always ready for a beer, Krog made a beeline for the car. It was close quarters in the front seat. He sat down on the seat with the cooler right in front of him. When he popped the lid off the cooler, he screamed and hit his head on the door jam on his way out of the car. I'm not sure whether the scream was because he hit his head or because of the snake. This deal broke everyone up for a few days. Krog was mighty careful after that whenever he opened any cooler.

While breeding for Hyland Angus and several of their neighbors in the Highmore-Ree Heights area, I met the gal who became my wife. Linda Hasart was riding heat detection for Tom Steers south of Ree Heights and I was doing AI for Tom. We met in the pasture and about a year later we were married. Coincidence is a funny thing. Clayton's wife Dorothy was a roommate of my mother-in-law in the Miller, South Dakota, hospital when both Clayton's daughter Gloria and my wife Linda were born.

Today we live on a place on the eastern side of the Black Hills of South Dakota that we purchased in 1971. This place was totally paid for by technician fees that I generated breeding cows for Hyland Angus and their neighbors. When my dad Rand was a teenager he visited the Black Hills. This must have been about 1932, and he fell in love with the area. He always said that he wanted to live and retire in the Black Hills. Hyland Angus made his dream become a reality and we are thankful for the good business that Clayton, Ted and Ron Jennings gave us over a long period of time.

L. M. "Doc" Cropsey, Phil VanDerVoort and Clayton Jennings in Phil's office at Piedmont, SD - 1995

Chapter 33

Bob-Tailed Heifers

In March of 1956 we experienced one of the most miraculous survivals of 160 first calf heifers with baby calves at side in the history of our ranch operation.

The cows were all coming two years old and all had a baby calf from ten days to thirty days old. We had good luck calving these pairs and we needed to get them out of the muddy calving yards to a clean pasture. We hoped to avoid calf scours and pneumonia or both.

We had lots of snow all winter long and now the weather turned exceptionally mild. Most of the snow on the prairie melted and the water ran down the creeks and into the dams in the pastures. Most of the dams were full to running over.

During this warm spell our Hyland Angus Ranch crew had sharp-shod two teams of horses. They also sharp-shod four of our top saddle horses as we knew we would need them to get through the muck in the cattle yards and calving areas.

On Monday March 25th, after we finished the morning chores I talked with my foreman, Bill Pender, and we decided to move the heifers and calves (that could travel) to a clean pasture about two miles southeast of our ranch headquarters. We thought it would be an ideal place as we hadn't used it much the year prior and the carry-over grass was from eight to ten inches tall and there was water everywhere. All we would need to do was supplement them with a jag of hay each day. There is nothing that looks better to a rancher than a thrifty set of new calves that have plenty of room in a dry area to run and jump and play. Likewise there is nothing more nauseating that a set of sick calves with ears hanging low and severe scours. Our theory at the ranch was to get all cow/calf pairs on clean pasture with plenty of water as soon as possible. There are times when it is an impossibility to get this done, but it is so vital to do your best always and take your rewards in the fall.

We headed the heifer/calf pairs to pasture right after lunch. We strung the heifers and calves out so they wouldn't bunch and start looking for their calves. We had exceptional luck all the way. The heifers walked slowly and their calves would run and catch up to them. Never had we had a string of pairs that moved so easily without mis-mating. Some days pairs like this move easily and some days it can be a real mess. We were lucky to have a good day for movement.

One of the cowboys on horseback rode ahead to the gate and opened it wide. Every heifer and every calf seemed to feel at home as they passed through the gate. We left them alone as soon as the last one had entered the gate.

About dark we rode among them on horseback and everything was fine. We rode back to the ranch and everyone of us had a good feeling that we had done a big job well.

The next morning we ran a check on the heifers and calves and they seemed to be as contented as old cows with old calves on them. The sun was shining and it was another mild day.

Wednesday morning was still mild but it started snowing big flakes around noon and by evening the area was covered with over four inches of snow. My cowboys and I talked about gathering the heifers and calves but decided that they would be better off where they were. By the next morning high winds and quickly dropping temperatures brought blizzard conditions to the area, blocking many roads in the county. Ice was freezing in the water tanks. We thought we'd better keep our saddle and work horses in the barn, fed and ready to go as soon as the storm subsided.

A typical South Dakota blizzard raged all day Wednesday. By the next morning the winds had gone down but it was bitter cold. We all met in the horsebarn a couple of hours before daylight. We tried to envision just where the storm could have bunched or scattered the heifers. At daylight we struck out across the prairie with the four saddle horses and a bobsled and team. We scattered across the pasture and headed south as we knew the strong northwest wind would have pushed the heifers southward. They would go with the wind.

When we got about a mile south we hit a four wire cross fence. We found groups of calves lying around the four inch fence posts. They were in a circle around the post and covered with snow. When we came upon them they would shake their heads and the snow would fly off. It was a sight I had never seen before or have I since. We found several breaks in the wire fence where the heifers had gone through heading south with the wind.

We left one of the guys with the team and sled to observe the calves and locate as many as he could. The four of us on horseback rode swiftly south. We spotted a group of heifers against a fence in a draw. These heifers were okay. We went on approximately one half mile further and came upon a dam. It was a sad sight, one that we were afraid could happen. As we rode closer to the dam we could see that a bunch of the heifers had drifted into the dam. All you could see of them was their head and nose sticking out and up from the ice. We could hardly distinguish them as they were all white from the driven snow. The ice had frozen around them. It looked like every heifer in the dam was frozen to death. The first thing Bill Pender did was kick one on the nose and she wriggled her head so we knew she still had life. We drew a sigh of relief. We went on to next few and did the same thing. We found each heifer would wriggle its head and shake the snow off. We knew we had to do something quick. We discovered that the heifer's bodies were not frozen in the dam, but we found that their tails was frozen out behind tight in the ice.

We each grabbed a rope that we always carried on the saddle and put it around a heifer's head like a halter. We pulled up and straight ahead, but no way could we pull her out because of her tail frozen solid in the ice.

Bill Pender said, "Boys, I've got a good sharp jackknife and I'll cut the tail off and the rest of you guys hoist her out."

We got ready to hoist her as soon as the tail came off and it was no easy job. It probably took a minute or more to cut the tail off as he was cutting it close to the body. Bill said "Okay" and we all hoisted. We got her front feet on the ice, dragged her forward and took the halter off. We watched her flounder for a couple minutes before she was able to get her feet under her. Then she shook her head and body and took a step or two at a time then walked on her own to the edge of the dam. We quickly used the same procedure on the next heifers - Bill Pender cutting the tails off and the rest of us hoisting them out. There were no injuries other than the blood on the tailhead. It took us a couple hours to get all the heifers out that had been trapped in the dam.

We gathered another bunch of heifers in another corner of the pasture. We decided that one of the guys should go back to the bobsled and help load the calves (about 20 at a time in the bobsled). The calves had found a little shelter and had lain down and the snow covered them over. They took them back to our pasture and waited with this first load until we could drive the heifers back. We would then unload the calves with the heifers and go get another load of the calves from the fenceline until we had them all paired up. We watched them as they paired up and it was a beautiful sight.

We took a load of really good green hay and scattered it for a quarter of a mile. They ate vigorously. We were able to get a really good count on them and we were truly pleased that every one of the heifers and calves were intact. We were able to leave them in this pasture until new grass time.

This was what I call a miracle as we had such good luck finding all the calves and getting the heifers out without any injuries except tailless. Sixty of the heifers had truly short tails, only about two or four inches left from the tailhead, but we culled them sharply for production and had none left after two or three years. A bob-tailed cow always shows up first in a herd and as many as we had it made an unusual sight. I would much prefer to have bob-tailed cows as no cows at all! This was as close to a catastrophe as I ever care to witness. We could have lost all the calves and part of the heifers if the storm had hung on much longer.

If you are lucky enough you don't need to be smart. We were truly lucky!

Bill and Fern Pender

Chapter 34

Let's Paint the West Black Sale

In the late 1950's Dave Canning and I talked about some extra promotion of Angus cattle to invade the vast Hereford numbers in the West.

We decided to have a "Let's Paint The West Black" sale in November and locate as central as possible, so we chose the stockyards sale barn at the National Western Stock Show facilities in Denver, Colorado.

Several Angus breeders volunteered to consign commercial Angus bred heifers as they were very much in demand all through the cattle country. There was much interest before sale time.

We had about 600 heifers consigned and we planned to sell them in carload lots only. All of our consignments were of superior quality. They were a fantastic set of females and the bidding was fast and crisp. For that time the price seemed extra good as they averaged $265.00 per head.

This sale served its purpose — we sold these heifers into five or six adjoining states and they made their mark in strong Hereford country.

We had a strong feeling that we were starting to "paint the west black"!

Dave Canning, sale manager, and Clayton Jennings examine a carlot of Jennings' Angus cows which topped the "Let's Paint the West Black" commercial sale in Denver, sold to Godley Bros., Elizabeth, Colorado

Jennings Brothers commercial Angus consignment to "Let's Paint the West Black" sale in Denver, Colorado

Chapter 35

Frances

In the late 1950's Stanley and Frances Johnston, neighboring ranchers, of Ree Heights, South Dakota, had a new litter of purebred white German Shepherd pups. These dogs were bred for sincerity and loyalty of little kids trying to grow up. Stanley and Frances wanted to give the pick of the litter to my children, Charlie, age eight, and Gloria Jean, age three.

Charlie, Gloria Jean and I went over to the Johnston Ranch when the pups were just big enough to wean. The children decided on a certain pup. She was snow white and had a unique personality. We named her Frances for Stanley's wife and she maintained that name from everyone who saw her. She grew into the most beautiful white dog anyone had ever seen.

We took Frances home with us in the car. First Gloria Jean and then Charlie took turns cuddling and petting their most precious possession of their lives.

When we got to the ranch the children made a home for her in our garage. She always waited for them to come outside to play. She dedicated herself at all times to the two children. As soon as they came out of the house she was their constant companion. She watched after them wherever they might wander on the ranch and protected them from harm at all times. If either of the children got in harm's way she would pull them back to safety.

One day the three of them wandered out to the stackyard where the men were stacking hay. Glenn Dawson, one of our top hands, thought he would test the loyalty, sincerity and courage of Frances. He grabbed Charlie by the arm in the pretense of harm and Frances went into action. She grabbed Dawson's pant leg and ripped it to shreds and frightened Dawson beyond explanation. It took a couple of our men who knew Frances well to pull her off Dawson before she could do any more harm.

1957 - Charlie Jennings, Frances and Gloria Jennings

From that day on, whenever Dawson came to the headquarter's ranch for any reason, he could not get out of his pickup because Frances was there snarling and showing her teeth in anticipation of further entanglement with him.

Fourth of July celebrations on the ranch were great fun for everyone except Frances. Because of her protectiveness, she would try to carry off popping strings of Black Cats. We were afraid she would be hurt so Frances always was locked up in the garage during the fireworks displays. She would frantically try to escape her prison, barking and jumping.

One day Frances led Charlie and Gloria Jean down to a big old corn crib near the corrals. She crawled under the corn crib and the two kids crawled under after her in a space that was barely big enough for them. In this small space, to their surprise, they found that Frances wanted to show them her litter of pups. She was so proud and it gave the children a great thrill.

Frances was without question one of the most important events and happenings of my children's young lives. They both loved this dog with all their hearts and the dog loved them equally - and it was an intensely sad day when Frances died. Both the children helped me bury her in the yard in the shade of a large spruce tree.

Frances truly was "Kids Best Friend"!

MEMORIES FROM KAROL PYKIET

My first memory of Clayton Jennings was when I was in the first grade. My parents and I were spending Easter Sunday at the Jennings' main ranch. We were visiting good friends Bud and Elinor Hahn. Most of the day had been spent outside with Gloria Jennings and Mike Hahn. Gloria and her family had a dog named Frances. She was a beautiful white German Shepherd. She was always with the kids when they were outside playing.

Frances had given birth to a large litter of pups a few weeks before and Clayton was anxious to find homes for them. I remember him asking me if I would like to take a puppy home. I said my parents might not want me to have one. I never was sure what Clayton said to convince them otherwise, but on that Sunday night I rode home with Mom and Dad with a puppy on my lap. I still can remember that warm feeling a child has when holding a soft cuddly puppy. I was a happy seven year old girl in the year 1957.

As I grew to know Clayton over the years, I found him to be a very giving man. There was never a time he didn't have a kind word or a smile for me. The same holds true today when I go to visit him. He is still giving back to family, friends, and his community. We all should be so lucky to know and appreciate his wonderful generosity.

Now 37 years later I am married with two children of my own. I have a seventeen year old son named Clayton Dean. A tribute to two men in my life who had a great influence on me - Clayton Jennings and my dad, Dean Branine. Clayton always teases my dad that he stands in second place. He still keeps his sense of humor.

Last Christmas I received for a gift from my brother and wife, Clayton's book "HANDSHAKE:Code of the West". I cried when I read what Clayton had written inside the cover. It brought back so many good memories of my childhood and the summer days I spent at the Jennings' Hyland Angus Ranch ranch.

1994 - Karol Branine Pykiet

Clayton Pykiet

Drew Pykiet

Chapter 36

June

June Olson, a widow lady who now lives in Highmore, has been both friend and neighbor since the 1940's. She and her husband Roy owned a good small ranch adjoining our south Hyland Angus Ranch on Peno road on Elm Creek.

Elm Creek is not a famous creek but is an asset to every ranch it runs through. It is a mild winding snakelike creek that meanders through a lot of ranches before it dumps into the Missouri River. It has lots of small shade trees on both sides of the creek that shelter the cattle in the summer from the heat and the cold winds and blizzards in the winter.

June Olson - 1993

We bought the Olson's calves and excess feed, which they had plenty of, every year. They were a real pleasure to work with on the deals we made with them. We bought their corn for silage, lots of oats, prairie hay and alfalfa hay. This excess feed sale to us gave them some loose money to do as they wished. They were never hard-nosed in their deals and we tried not to be hard-nosed with them. They were just good people - salt of the earth people - honest and dependable.

Occasionally a few of our commercial cattle would stray into their pasture. We expected our neighbors to

Elm Creek - one of the few times the creek went out of its banks and filled the valley - Spring of 1952

call us about our cattle if they drifted onto their ranches - WE EXPECTED THAT! But Olson's would gather any of our strays in the fall before selling time and drive them by saddle horse down Elm Creek to our ranch headquarters. They wanted no money, but they would accept thanks - that is what I say is salt of the earth people!

They were always good extra help when we started gathering our cattle for shipment in the fall. They seemed to enjoy working with our crews and they were really fun people. It has always been quite evident that June is a workaholic and no job is too hard or too long for her. She can do any work any man can do anytime.

One fall day when I was looking at their excess feed that I planned to buy they asked me to stay for dinner. The food was plentiful and really good. I bragged on the beef being so good several times and then June said, "Well it ought to be good because it is one of your steers!" Then she laughed like crazy. At first, I wasn't sure if she meant it or not. Then I recognized that she was using a little reverse psychology on me as I was aware she would rather give than receive.

Thank God for good neighbors and we had many!

Chapter 37

All American Romance

I happened to have a very good friend, Cliff Spencer, in Great Falls, Montana. He had spotted and bought many carloads of feeder cattle for the Jennings Brothers in his area during the late 50's. Basically he was a sheep man by trade and one of the most potent sheep dealers in the whole west, but he did spot cattle for us.

During the cattle shipping season he either called me or I called him almost every night. During one of these phone conservations he said, "Clayt, I want you to come up to Great Falls and meet a certain girl!" From then on every time we talked he wanted to know when I was coming to Great Falls as he had this girl he wanted me to meet, but he wouldn't tell me a thing about her.

Calvin Gadd, a good friend and neighbor of mine, was driving for me at the time. It made it so much easier to have a friend help me drive and alert me on people and livestock. I had several bunches of cattle to look at in the Billings, Lewistown, Roundup and Harlowtown areas. We thought we could do it in one day if we got out early in the morning. We drove to Billings and spent the night. We got up very early and we were able to make all the stops and bought about half a trainload of cattle.

Calvin Gadd - 1985

I informed Cliff Spencer that we would be in Great Falls late the next afternoon. He said that he had to be sorting and loading sheep and wouldn't be able to meet us. But he gave me a number to call as soon as I got to Great Falls. He told me her name was Ramona Haeh. I called the number that Cliff had given me and a lovely voice answered. I asked if she was Ramona Haeh. She told me no, but she would put her right on the phone.

When Ramona said "Hello" in a slow drawl, I knew that she was an unusual human being. It seemed that we were both anticipating our first meeting. She asked me where I was and I told her I had just checked into the best hotel in town. She said, " Great, I'm anxious to meet you." I responded, "Why don't I pick you up and we'll go out to dinner"? I asked her who the girl was who had answered the phone and she told me that she was her best girlfriend. I said, "I've got my best friend with me. Why don't we hook the two of them up?" Ramona said she had a car and they would meet the two of us in the hotel lobby at 8 o'clock.

Cal and I got ready and dressed the best we could and when they arrived we were waiting for them in the hotel lobby. When they came in we didn't know which was which. They came right up to us as if we were long time friends. One was quite a little taller than the other, simply because she had on five inch spike heels, which were the fad of the day. She also had on a beautiful green velveteen dress that quivered when she walked that would excite any or all of the male species. Then everything blended.

Ramona had made reservations for dinner for the four of us in the most elegant dining room I had ever seen. We had a cocktail and a luscious dinner. Then we danced, changing partners every other dance. Cal's date was a very charming girl. She was a graceful dancer and lots of fun. We all agreed that we had a wonderful evening.

Cal and I walked the girls back to their car and on the way along the hotel were some steel grates in the sidewalk. As we were crossing them Ramona caught her five inch heel in the grate and broke it off and with another step she broke off the other one. That made her heel-less. The four of us laughed so much and so loud that we could have been heard a mile away. That incident and the way she graciously accepted it made me know I was with a bigtime gal.

The car was most of a block away and we laughed and made fun all the way. When we reached the car it was mind boggling, as it was the biggest, blackest, newest Cadillac in the business. It shone like a monkey's heel. We put the gals in the car without even a kiss, but we told them we were going to stay over a day or two and we would call them tomorrow. If I would have wanted to kiss her with the spike heels on I would have had to stand on my tiptoes or on a doorstep with her on the level.

The next morning Ramona called me about seven o'clock. She wondered if Cal and I would go with her up to her ranch north of Great Falls nearly to the Canadian border. She would pick us up at the hotel in short order. I told her we would be waiting for her in the hotel lobby. She drove up in her big black Cadillac. There was a good hardtop road all the way to the ranch. We enjoyed the beauty of that country. She drove real swiftly, probably seventy or eighty miles an hour, but it was smooth. She pulled into her ranch home and we went in with her for coffee, pop or what-have-you.

She showed us her home in its entirety. Each bedroom had a queen or king sized bed and everything in the house was immaculate and beautiful. The most dazzling sight in the whole house, which was absolutely beautiful was a U-shaped counter in the

Ramona Haeh and a mountain sheep she shot - 1957

kitchen. But the most striking feature was an over-hanging wooden rack on the contour of the counter. It was about eight or ten yards in length and hanging from this rack by the handles were about every size pot and pan and every one had a copper bottom. The copper bottomed pots and pans matched perfectly Ramona's copper colored hair.

Ramona was a fantastic big game hunter. She loved to hunt deer, elk, moose, bear, and most every type of game bird. She had personally shot all of the trophies mounted on the beautiful knotty pine walls of her trophy room. She had two large glass enclosed gun racks that held 20 or more guns of every calibre.

After we had sipped coffee and laughed and told jokes, Ramona said she needed our help to take a litter of pups into Great Falls to the veterinarian to get their shots as she wanted to wean them. We both said, "We're ready to help you anytime!"

We went out and got into the car, but before we were to get the pups she wanted to give us a tour of her ranch. We drove up a dirt trail a couple miles or more and we saw a pumping oil well. She told us she had eighteen of these pumping oil wells - not gushing but good ones. This left Cal and I nearly breathless.

She said she could easily keep herself busy on this ranch but she also had a car rental service in Sacramento, California, that kept her busy besides running back and forth between California and Montana. Later we found that her car rental was the largest agency in all of California. She was very modest in telling about herself and her business. If Cal and I ever had a tendency to develop an inferiority complex this was the time and place.

After spending an hour or more up the dirt trails and back, Ramona suggested that we better get the pups and take them to Great Falls. She pulled up by an elegant dog house. She had a big rubber tub about 2 feet long and ten inches deep to put the pups in. The mama dog was a purebred Black Lab dog and she had eight puppies. We put the black tub on the floor of the backseat and it fit nicely. We put the mama dog on the seat just back of the pups. Ramona said, "Cal, you get in the back seat and Clayton you sit in the front seat with me." So away we went, heading for the vet shop in Great Falls one hour or more away.

As we drove along it was all smiles, laughter and jokes until we got about half way to Great Falls, when the pups starting yelping and puking. They were getting carsick. Soon our smiles and laughter subsided. The pups continued to yelp and puke, until the odor got so bad that none of us could stand it any longer. We turned down all the windows, turned around and headed back to the ranch. The odor was such a god-awful odor for anyone to experience. The mama dog just sat there and did nothing.

We finally arrived back at the ranch and pulled up to an outside faucet that had a hose attached.

Ramona said, "Get the pups close to the hydrant and I'll get some towels."

She went into the house and returned with some beautiful extra large white towels and some liquid soap. She soaped them down good and rinsed them off. Then she handed them to Cal and me and we dried them as best as we could with the oversized white towels. We both came out looking like we'd had a bath as the pups shook and sprayed water all over us. The stress had been enough for the pups so we decided to wait for another day to take them to the vet.

I can't describe, so just imagine, how the back seat and floor of Ramona's car looked and smelled. We sprayed water on the entire back seat and floor board, let it dry and vacuumed until it was nearly back to normal. Then we headed back to Great Falls. We took side roads so Ramona could explain some of the wonders of her country.

We spent another fun evening in Great Falls. Then Cal and I had to get home. The next time that I saw Ramona was at the 1958 Rose Bowl game in Pasadena, California.

On the long drive home I dreamed about Ramona. My first impression of her had been that of a Greek goddess. She had more beauty and feminine attributes than I had ever witnessed anytime or anyplace. Her proportions were absolutely not measurable. She had long wavy copper colored hair that waved like a windsock in the breeze. Her face was light in color with well-placed freckles. Her lips were full and ruby red and very expressive. Her voice was soft and gentle. Her manners were elegant and most convincing. She had a graceful walk in her five inch high heels that make her taller than I, but it mattered not as it was the thing of the day.

In January of 1958 Cecil Ice of Ice Flying Service, Pierre, South Dakota, flew me out to Pasadena, California, for the Rose Bowl game between Ohio State and Oregon. Ramona had reservations at a hotel in Beverly Hills for herself and me. Ramona drove her car down from Sacramento and met Cecil and me at the hotel. We took her car to the football game. We parked at least a mile from the Rose Bowl. Ramona told us that in order to see the parade we should walk and see the floats lining up. It surely was worth the walk as it was a sensational sight to see. She was professionally inclined. What a woman!

Ramona had two tickets for us at the Rose Bowl game on the 45 yard line about 30 rows up. There were no better seats in the Rose Bowl that held a little over one hundred thousand people. She didn't know that Cecil would be going to the game with us so she didn't have a ticket for him. I went out near the stadium and scalped him a ticket. During the game a man sitting in the seat next to Cecil had a seizure. He fell on Cecil's lap and died immediately. It was a scary situation for Cecil and when he told us about it, it was quite unbelievable.

That evening the three of us went out to one of the fanciest restaurants in Hollywood. We enjoyed a cocktail or two and a delicious dinner. We danced to a fancy dance band. The whole evening was filled with fun and laughter and fulfillment. The next morning Ramona left for Sacramento and Cecil and I started our hedge-hop home. This was one of the most beautiful experiences of my life.

Some time later, Ramona called me one evening at my ranch. She said she had a couple of days to spare and would like to come visit me at my ranch in South Dakota. I said, "Come tomorrow and I'll be waiting for you at the ranch". It was a long way from Great Falls to the Hyland Angus Ranch, probably a thousand to eleven hundred miles. She said she could make it in a full day. I didn't doubt that she could, because I had ridden with her in that big black Cadillac at 75 or 80 miles an hour and it seemed like we were just coasting.

Ramona pulled into my ranch yard in the late afternoon. She got out of the car and we embraced with a glorious kiss. I was most happy to see her and it seemed mutual.

We spent the rest of the afternoon riding around my ranch in my pickup. We saw lots of our registered Angus cows and calves. We pulled in to my yard and I escorted her into the front door that led to my classy western sun room. I told her to look around the sun room and I would get us a little highball. I knew what she liked and I mixed mine the same.

When I was single with two small children on the ranch, I hired Mrs. Irene Smithers, a 60 year old widowed lady, to come and live with us during the summers. She always took good care of Charlie and Gloria. She was so dependable - she really loved the kids. Never did I worry when I was gone for several days or a week at a time.

Mrs. Smithers prepared Ramona and I a delicious roast beef dinner. She retired to her room as soon as she had the kitchen cleaned up. My children were spending a few days with my sister, Nadine, in Miller. Finally Ramona and I were alone. I gave her a tour of my rambling ranch-style home. We wandered from room to room hand-in-hand. She said, "Clayton, I'm going to stay another day." And she did. We talked about marriage and we both wondered if "black crude oil" would mix with "Black Angus cattle". We were both sure that they would mix, but the main obstacle was whose life would have to change. She was truly busy taking care of all her

Charlie, Clayton and Gloria Jennings - 1958

Gloria Jennings on her horse and Mrs. Smithers on the bicycle in front of the Hyland Angus Ranch home - 1957

business ventures. She was totally consumed of time and loved every minute of it very much. Likewise I had more business deals than I could keep up with as I was hedge-hopping by private plane on cattle buying and selling deals all over the United States, Canada, and old Mexico. I also had a ranch to run.

We decided that we would go along a while like we were as neither of us felt like we wanted to give up our businesses. We would set a date by phone, making arrangements to meet whenever we could. I want to say now for Ramona and myself that we were in total ecstasy of every minute of every hour of every day whenever we were together. We were always able to arrange a get-together at some place or other. Two occasions were in consecutive years at the Rose Bowl games in Pasadena. She always made all the arrangements - hotel, tickets for the game, and lavish evening dinners and dances.

When she left my ranch for her home, we had a very good understanding. Both of us were single and could do whatever we desired. We did talk a couple of times a week and if we missed a time then we would talk an hour or more catching up on everything.

Ramona and I attended the January 1959 Rose Bowl game when Iowa defeated California. The morning after the game she called me quite early and asked me if I had a bathing suit. I told her that I didn't bring one along as I didn't think we would be swimming at that time of year.

She said, "Well, I'm going to put mine on and we'll grab one for you along the way. We're going to go swimming in the Pacific Ocean."

When she knocked on my hotel door she was wearing her suit with a kimono over it. She also had a couple large towels from her hotel room. We got into her big black Cadillac and drove down the street. She stopped at the first store that carried men's clothing. We went in and I grabbed the first pair of swim trunks that I saw. I went into the men's room and put them on. We hurried to the car and headed for Malibu Beach.

When we got to the beach, we parked and locked the car. We took a blanket and the towels and walked down to the beach. Ramona embraced me and said, "Isn't this wonderful, Clayton?"

She then stepped back, dropped her kimono and started running down the beach in the beautiful soft sand. When she was about ten yards away I started after her. She ran like a gazelle, so graceful and swift and everything else! She had freckles on every inch of her body that I could see, which was most of her body as she had on not much more than a G-string. This was the keenest physique of the female species I had ever witnessed. She ran quite a ways along the beach. Then she stopped suddenly and turned around. I ended up in her arms. We were both out of wind from running so hard. We clung to each other and had a long lasting kiss. This episode I will remember all the rest of my life simply because it still remains vividly in my mind after thirty-six years. Then we ran hand-in-hand into the ocean. Some would call the water chilly, but I would call it darn cold! We had a quick swim. Then we headed back to the hotel.

The next day both of us returned to our businesses, but before we parted we verified that we were each free to keep on seeing each other until we married.

The real reason that I did not commit myself to Ramona was that I was looking for someone who would help me raise my two young children, Charlie and Gloria. I also desired married life. I was sick of being single. I had been dating a gal on occasion in Denver. She was a secretary and she was Eloise Dwyer. I married Eloise in Denver in March of 1959.

My marriage to Eloise ended my "All American Romance" with Ramona, but I did see her one more time and that was at the National Western Stock Show in Denver in 1960. Eloise and I had a suite of rooms at the Cosmopolitan Hotel. I invited Ramona to bring her husband for a visit at our suite - and she did. Ramona's husband was big in oil and steel and you know that Ramona was big in oil, car rentals, ranching and Cadillacs. It seems as though the four of us had a very nice visit. I never saw Ramona again.

Chapter 38

South American Trip - 1960

I was attending the National Western Stock Show in Denver in January 1960. There I met Lee Leachman, a good friend of mine from Ankony Angus of Rhinebeck, New York. He talked to me about a big livestock exposition in Argentina, which was rated as the most prestigious livestock show in South America. Lee had sold numerous champion Angus bulls to the aristocracy of Argentina and it would be a great opportunity for us to meet and see the top Angus breeding herds and foremost cattlemen on the Pampa of Argentina.

We were to meet Lee in Buenos Aires in September 1960 where this exposition took place. Lee would take care of all the arrangements for our stay in Buenos Aires. I told him I would have to let him know if my wife Eloise and I could make it. He said he knew I would be absolutely amazed at the show and showings.

Eloise and I talked it over. We felt it was a distinct privilege to have such a distinguished Angus breeder invite us to the most prestigious livestock show in South America. We accepted his invitation and agreed to meet him in Buenos Aires in September.

Our home at that time was the Hyland Angus Ranch at Highmore, South Dakota. We had consistent rains during the spring and summer of 1960 making the volunteer bluegrass come up all over the prairie on our ranch. Bluegrass is a bonus money crop that we get every so often in this part of the country. We had stripped bluegrass a couple years prior and it paid really well. At this time, all of our ranch help were busy taking out crops and hay so my wife Eloise volunteered herself and a girl who worked for us, Marlene Newman from Montana, to strip the bluegrass.

The bluegrass companies furnished the strippers. Strippers are small circular rotating machines pulled by small tractors that strip the seeds out of the blugrass heads. We furnished the two light tractors that pulled four or six strippers at one time. They could cover a lot of prairie ground in a short time. The girls worked from daylight till dark. Then after dark they took the seed to Wilbur's Feed and Seed Company in Miller. They had to work hard and fast as the bluegrass stripping only lasted about a week. If a stripper broke down, you didn't fix it, you just unhooked it from the rest of the machines and left it sitting in the pasture. Time is of the essence. If a strong South Dakota wind comes along that is the end of the stripping as the seeds all blow out of the heads and onto the ground. When the stripping was done, Eloise took the balance of the seed into Miller and came home with a check for $3870.00. It didn't take us long to say, "Let's make that a three week trip to South America!" We could meet Lee in Buenos Aires while we were on our tour of South America.

Eloise and I set up a tour so we could visit several of the prominent cities in South America. We flew out of Pierre, South Dakota, to Miami, Florida. From there we were to fly into Caracas, Venezuela, but Americans were not in much favor there for some political reason. The Venezuelans had been bombarding the tourists as they got off their planes in Caracas with ripe and rotten tomatoes. We thought this would be messy, so we cancelled that part of the trip and flew on to Rio de Janeiro, Brazil. We found a guide and toured the city of Rio and found it to be fascinating and unusual. We spent the night and then flew to Sao Paulo, Brazil.

Sao Paulo was the largest industrial city in South America. It was one of the most beautiful cities in the world and also one of the most crowded. The main industry was assembly plants for many American and foreign vehicles. Men from all over the world congregated there as they knew they could find employment. Sao Paulo was called the "melting pot" of the entire world.

We checked into our hotel and hired a guide. We always had a guide as they could translate for us and they knew all the interesting places to see. He took us around all the industrial and residential areas of the city. In the evening we took our guide to dinner with us so we could learn more about Brazil.

While eating dinner he suggested that he take us out and show us one of the most unusual sights of the world "the girls in glass". We tried to find out what this sight might be, but he evaded telling us for some time. Finally he said it was one of the largest places of prostitution in the world, only Singapore and HongKong could compare. It was quite a surprise to us, but we agreed that we should probably see this place. He did say that no women were allowed on the street, but he knew he could get Eloise in with a little green money. There is always a way.

We finished our dinner and left with our guide. He had his own car and he drove us to an area near the industrial part of Sao Paulo. He parked his car on the cobblestone street and told us he would be right back. He returned with two policemen with whom he had arranged for them to take us in the area which was about one city block wide and two city blocks long. He tipped the policemen $20.00 each and they were our personal escorts where ever we went.

The area was a solid mass of men of all ages and all nationalities. They were milling around and watching the performance. On the far side of this entire area of two blocks long was a brick building about a story and a half high. There were stairways going in on the side of the building. At the top of the building there were 20' long by 7' high bay windows the full length of the building where the girls would parade past the windows and down the other end to the lower level. There was every description of girls - tall girls, fat girls, skinny girls, big girls, and little girls from beautiful to homely. Some wore beautiful long gowns, some dressed modern, some wore very short dresses, and some had on scanties.

There were no less than 2000 of the male species there that evening. The girls walked slowly just one time in front of the window and if a man wanted the girl and he was quick enough he went into the stairway.

All the while as we walked through this section with the cops we meandered through the crowd of men and close to the windows. We were very nervous to see so much humanity and feel the anticipation as we walked through the crowd. We walked the full length of the building and never saw the same girl twice. We probably watched for a half hour. We were shocked and surprised at the immensity of this house of prostitution.

We got back to the hotel and discussed this situation with our guide over a cup of coffee. He said this district was owned and operated by the city of Sao Paulo. It was run twenty-four hours a day. There was almost no crime or major problems associated with it. Sex crimes were practically non-existent in the city. This was the only way the city could survive.

1960 - Bar in Buenos Aires , ? , ? , Jorge Ezcurra, Eloise and Clayton Jennings

1960 - Bar in Buenos Aires, Tom Adams milking, Eloise Jennings, Clayton Jennings, Herman Purdy (behind Eloise)

The next morning we flew to Buenos Aires, Argentina, which is a very beautiful city with broad avenues, numerous parks and plazas making it look spacious and tranquil. The Avenda 9 de Julio is 425' wide making it the widest street in the world.

Lee Leachman met us at the airport. He had plans for us for our entire stay of five or six days. Lee made us acquainted with many of the aristocracy of the cattle industry. A lot of them were real cattle barons who owned vast amounts of land, cattle and horses. It was definitely a broadening of our experiences with land and cattle.

They took us out and showed us many ranches and many good cattle. We flew in their private planes from Buenos Aires to their individual ranches. They were very gracious people and seemed to be very happy to have us as their guests and would not let us pay for anything under any circumstance. We went to the show a couple of days and watched the placing of the champions. It was very impressive and exciting. The enthusiasm was as great or greater than at any of the shows we had witnessed in America. They seemed to cherish any ribbon or trophy that they won with their livestock. This show at Buenos Aires was rated as one of the largest in the world.

We flew from Buenos Aires to Iquito, Peru, arriving there toward evening. The hotel management recommended a guide for us. We told him we had one day and we would like to see Peru. He said we couldn't see it in one day but he could take us on one good trip in a day. He explained that it was a trip by a motor launch fifty miles or more down the Amazon River. He verified that we could leave the next morning and we would get back by dark. He would arrange for something to eat during the trip, but for us to prepare for a long hot trip as we were near the equator. We needed to have a light-weight hat, long sleeves and light gloves. Eloise had brought with us several pair of light-weight gloves and several hats. The sun would shine and it would get really hot. It sounded like a worthwhile trip and we agreed to be ready at the hotel the next morning.

Our guide met us at daylight the next morning in the hotel lobby. He would take us to the river and pick us up that evening on our return. It was a regular excursion for visitors like us. We thought we were prepared adequately for the trip but found we could have done better in our wearing apparel. The river was very smooth when we started off, no ruffles or waves what-so-ever. The river widened to two miles or more. There was dense jungle on

1960 - Clayton and Eloise Jennings landing in Peru

each side of the river. About the only signs of life was an occasional native village. It was hot and very humid when we started and got consistently hotter as we went along. When it became high noon we found out what hot was. Had we not been covered with the hats, gloves and sleeves we would have burned to a crisp. It was heat and humidity like we had not experienced before.

We stopped at one of the native villages situated along the river bank. The natives were waiting for us. They had their wares and trinkets ready to sell. We bought some souvenirs to bring home. We enjoyed the trip as we spent a day on the largest river in the world. We learned lots that we didn't know before, but did not have the desire to do it ever again.

Our guide was waiting for us as we docked. He took us back to the hotel and we made arrangements with him to take us to the airport the next morning.

We flew out of Iquito the next morning headed for Bogota, Columbia, the drug capital of the world. Anyway that's what our guide told us. Bogota is high in the Andes Mountains with much of the city surrounded by steep mountains giving it a dramatic setting. On one high peak you can see a figure of Christ, on another a cross and on a third a shining white convent. Our highly educated guide made our stay in Bogota very enjoyable.

We flew out of Bogota for our last significant stop on our trip. We were headed for Mexico City. Eloise and I had decided to see a real "live to the death" bullfight between a matador and a bull. The world's largest bullfighting arena is Plaza de Toros Monumental in Mexico City. It seats fifty thousand persons.

We arrived in Mexico City and got a room at the largest hotel. We arranged for a guide to take us to the bullfight the next day.

That evening we thought we would like to stroll around the streets of Mexico City and see how the people lived. We had walked around two or three blocks when a small Mexican boy, probably 10 years old, slipped in front of us and we had to stop. He could speak some English but not much. He reached into his pockets and had something in each hand. He motioned for us to look and handed us two small boxes. We were somewhat startled, but the boy was so courteous and cute that we were willing to look. In one box was a beautiful gold wristwatch and in the other was a matched set of gold rings. The street was not well lighted but the watch and rings glittered in the semi-darkness. He made it clear he wanted to sell them to us. We had the feeling they were a real bargain at the price he asked, as he could say "real gold" and "cheap" very well. He showed us two more watches, similar to the first one, and he put on quite an act. We bought the four watches and two rings for less than $100.00. He was about as smooth a salesman, of any age, I had encountered in my life. This was a real business for him and he had a good business with a lot of people like us walking the streets.

When we got back to the room we looked everything over closely and they looked like the real McCoy, but a couple weeks after we got home everything started to tarnish and turn green. Everything we had bought was 100% phony.

We learned a lesson from that ten year old kid in Mexico City. "All that glitters is not gold!"

Our guide met us the next morning in the lobby of the hotel. Nearly every guide we had on the trip paid us handsomely by keeping us informed about everything as we went along. The guides always knew all the ins and outs of any predicament we might get into.

We took a cab from downtown Mexico City to the arena. We were in heavy traffic of humanity of 50,000+ people planning to attend the bullfight. They were going in every direction imaginable. There were lots of little Mexican boys near the arena who would polish your shoes for whatever you wanted to give them. We stopped for a quick shine on our boots.

This was a mob going to the bullfight. There was lots of hustle and bustle. Everyone was talking and shouting but we couldn't understand a word of it. We were so glad we had our guide to keep us informed about everything that was happening.

We got to our seats about half an hour before the bullfight. They were relatively good, up 30 or 40 rows from the arena. We could see easily everything that was happening. We had lots of time to listen to the Mexicans talk which seemed to float all around us.

Our guide explained to us the spectacle we were about to witness. He told us that the bull would be killed and the matador would be praised. Seldom is it that the matador gets injured or killed. There are three main acts in a bullfight. First the picador on a horse jabs the bull in the neck with a lance. This weakens the bull's neck muscles, causing the bull to charge with a lowered head. The picador's horse wears a blindfold and quilted padding. Then enters the banderilleros, on foot. They place three pair of darts in the muscles behind the bull's neck. The darts are mounted on shafts about two and one half feet long. The matador then enters alone and on foot. He is dressed in an elaborate silk costume trimmed with gold braid, sequins and beads. He carries a sword and a muleta, a small red cloth draped over a stick. He attracts the color-blind bull by shaking the muleta. The matador is the star of the afternoon. He usually kills two bulls in an afternoon.

This was nauseating to me. This was supposed to be a work of art and a great sport where you knew the answer before the end result. Each time the bull made a pass at the matador the crowd of 50,000 went absolutely wild. The noise was unbelievable. Eloise and I left with mixed feelings, but we knew one thing for certain we did not want to see another bullfight.

We had three beautiful and educational weeks in South America and Mexico, but we came home loving South Dakota all the more!

Chapter 39

International Beef Breeders

In 1958 my good friend at Raona Farms, Ray Smith informed me that Raona Farms had been sold to a successful engineer by the name of William L. Brittain. He was going to change the name to Mahogany Farms and keep Ray Smith as manager. Paul Good of Van Wert, Ohio, an auctioneer friend of mine, managed the transfer of this famous herd.

Bill Brittain, Ray Smith and Doc Cropsey had many long discussions on the future of beef cattle and the use of artificial insemination on a large scale, based on the many successes of AI at the Hyland Angus Ranch. They made plans to set up an AI organization near Denver.

In the summer of 1960, Ted and I with Brittain, VanDervoort, Cropsey and Ray Smith invested in a company to become known as International Beef Breeders (IBB). Bill Brittain's long-time partner at Hoover Ball and Bearing, Cliff Simmons, invested at the same time. Cliff is the father of Steve Simmons, the owner of Omega Farms at Williamston, Michigan, which includes the former Raona and Grand River Angus Farms.

An office was set up in Denver for this new organization. Doc Cropsey and Rand VanDervoort moved to Colorado. The semen to be used by IBB was to be collected at the Northern Illinois Breeders Coop. All of the semen to be used at IBB would be frozen. Hyland Angus Ranch sent several bulls to the Northern Illinois Breeders Coop to be collected and frozen. One of the bulls was Dor Macs Bardoliermere 24th who became a great semen producer and was very popular with many commercial Angus breeders.

In the spring of 1961 we had 30,000 units of frozen semen. The IBB organization with Doc Cropsey as president, was ready to hire temporary inseminators for the spring and summer breeding season. We bred many thousands of cattle in South Dakota, Idaho, Montana, Wyoming, Colorado and Nebraska. It was a very successful first year start.

In the fall of 1961, the Board of Directors of IBB decided that we needed to build a permanent headquarters in Colorado. We decided to sell more corporate shares of stock to cattlemen only. Nick Petry operated the Grizzly Ranch at Walden, Colorado. Nick also had a prominent construction company in Colorado so we welcomed him to do the land acquisition as well as the construction of the new headquarters at 136th Ave and I-25, just north of Denver. With Nick's ability and resources to speed up construction, the first bulls arrived at IBB right after the Denver Stock Show in January 1962.

Ted and I sent several bulls to IBB for semen collection as did Bill Brittain from his Mahogany Farms. Ankony Farms also sent some of their bulls. We also collected semen from Hereford and Charolois.

Many well-known cattlemen became corporate stockholders of IBB, such as Lee and Les Leachman and Myron Fuerst Ankony Farms, New York; John Quirk, Sr. and Kenneth Morrison, Hastings, Nebraska; Carlo Paterno, Meadow Lane Farms, New York; Max Fulscher, Amherst, Colorado; Wilbur May, Double Diamond Ranch,

Reno, Nevada; Dan and Harold Kissler, Bennett, Colorado; Herman Purdy, Penn State University; J. J. (Bud) Prosser, Longmont, Colorado; and Robert Purdy, Buffalo, Wyoming.

The new directors were Wilkie Collins of Morrison & Quirk, Bud Prosser, Herman Purdy, and Robert Purdy. Doc Cropsey was the chief operating officer and president. We were fortunate to obtain the services of Bud Prosser as laboratory manager. He was well-trained and experienced from Colorado State University. We were also fortunate to hire Wanda Pitman as secretary. She carried a big load and was the mainstay of the office. She was very efficient and became very knowledgeable in the AI business.

The whole staff at IBB was ready for a big year in 1962 and it was! Both Ted and I convinced many breeders in South Dakota and other states that they should use our services by purchasing supplies and semen, and then start their own insemination program. IBB also held AI training schools of one week in Denver. Many of my rancher friends attended these schools and did their own inseminating successfully.

I was proud to be a director of IBB for my ten years of ownership. Doc Cropsey and I became even closer friends as he spent many nights in my home during the AI breeding season. We also enjoyed many trips together, especially to Bill Britain's modern feed yard where 25 steers by each IBB sire were fed out for feed efficiency and carcass cut-out evaluation. A progeny test in the 60's that no one else was approaching as thoroughly as Mahogany Farms test center accomplished with Jerry Haarer as manager.

With IBB's phenomenal growth, as the first successful beef AI station in North America, it was obvious that there would be interest by some larger corporations to purchase it. In 1970 it was the decision of the Board of Directors of IBB to sell, "lock, stock and barrel" to the Syntex Pharmaceutical Firm at Palo Alto, California. Everyone who invested in IBB made a profit. It was a very enjoyable 10 year experience to be a part of the trend to breed better cattle for the future by using artificial insemination.

1962 - New Home of International Beef Breeders north of Denver, Colorado

L. M. "Doc" Cropsey in his office at International Beef Breeders, Denver, Colorado - 1961

Wanda Pitman, secretary for International Beef Breeders, Denver, Colorado - 1961

Denver - Doc and Mrs. Cropsey, Dr. and Mrs. Becky, Jim and Mrs. Wulf, Curtis Brown and Clayton Jennings. Reserve Champion Angus Carload of Steers sired by Tycoon. 1967 National Western Stock Show.

INTERNATIONAL BEEF BREEDERS

136th Avenue & North Washington Street
P.O. Box 29007   Denver, Colorado 80229
Phone 466-7353   Area Code 303

FROZEN SEMEN PRICE LIST

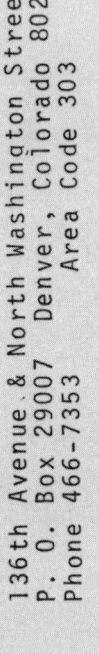

ANGUS HERD SIRES
- $7.00 – 601 Ballot of Belladrum
- 3.00 – 602 Mole's Hill Maximilian 1205
- 3.00 – 605 Mole's Hill Maximilian 124
- 2.00 – 609 Dor-Mac's Bardoliermere 24
- 4.00 – 611 Glencarnock Brigadier 30
- 2.00 – 612 Sugar Loaf Scot 913
- 3.00 – 613 Ankonian Astronaut
- 3.00 – 618 Glencarnock Bardoliermere 6
- 4.00 – 627 Ankonian Galahad
- 3.00 – 628 Ankonian Panarama 20
- 2.00 – 629 Mr. Marshall
- 3.00 – 630 Woodlawn Bardoliermere 106
- 2.00 – 634 Diamond Gambler
- 2.00 – 637 Mahogany Ballot 32
- 2.00 – 638 Valiant Bardolier
- 2.00 – 651 Meadow Lane Mystic

RED ANGUS HERD SIRE
- $2.00 – 902 Beckton Lakoto 201 HB-499

HEREFORD HERD SIRES
- $2.00 – 705 Majestic Silver 142
- 2.00 – 706 KB Nonsuch 243
- 3.00 – 708 Lucky Advance Lad
- 3.00 – 709 Princeton 23
- 2.00 – 713 Lucky Britisher H63
- 2.00 – 714 Lucky Real Blanchard
- 3.00 – 715 Princeton 15
- 3.00 – 716 Princeton 14
- 2.00 – 723 Beau Merit
- 5.00 – 724 Princeton

POLLED HEREFORD HERD SIRES
- $3.00 – 801 PS Pawnee Mixer 162
- 3.00 – 803 Bay Tontine 27

CHAROLAIS HERD SIRES
- $10.00 – 101 Amigo (Recordation use, includes semen transfer)
- 4.00 – 101 Amigo (Commercial use)
- 5.00 – 102 MGM Uncle Ed (Recordation)
- 2.50 – 102 MGM Uncle Ed (Commercial)
- 2.00 – 103 FWT Walhalla 710

International Beef Breeders semen list - 1963

IBB sires used artificially have produced the following Champion Carloads of Steers:

Grand Champion, International, 1969
Reserve Gr. Ch., International, 1968
Grand Champion, International, 1967
Grand Champion, American Royal, 1966
Grand Champion, International, 1965
Grand Champion, American Royal, 1965
Reserve Gr. Ch., International, 1964
Grand Champion, National Western, 1964
Grand Champion, International, 1963
Grand Champion, American Royal, 1963
Grand Champion, National Western, 1962
Grand Champion, National Western, 1961

International Beef Breeder Champions

Chapter 40

600 Purebred Angus Heifers

Hyland Angus Ranch had a good working relationship with many purebred Angus breeders east of the Mississippi. We bought many of these breeders crop of bulls each year and brought them west to South Dakota for development and resale to ranches in most all of the states west of the Missouri River. We developed a super demand and trade for Angus breeding bulls.

Hyland Angus Ranch had developed a large superior herd of registered Angus cows by keeping the top females every year. We had been using artificial insemination for several years and it had been showing up in the overall herd in quality and volume. The word got around all over America that we had the most uniform and top quality cows.

In 1962 Bill Brittain, owner of Mahogany Farms of Michigan and Ankony out of New York inquired about buying some of our registered cows. They wondered if we would be willing to sell 600 top-quality, extremely uniform running age cows. These two breeders got together and decided to buy 600 cows and divide them. It made us happy that two such high calibre breeders wanted to buy our cows.

They wanted to use this extensively bred, uniform group of purebred cows of known capabilities for experimental purposes for the evaluation of herd sires that would be in the International Beef Breeders Stud north of Denver.

It was pleasant and smooth in making the sale to these breeders. The cows had two different destinations so the cows had to be sorted before they were to be shipped — 300 to Mahogany Farms and 300 to Ankony. They each agreed to send a representative to help sort the cows. We were to ship them all by train on a date satisfactory with them both — which was probably a couple weeks. I also agreed to send a man with the train to see that the cows were fed, watered and rested at the feeding station in Chicago.

Early 1960's - Jim Donahue and Jerry Haarer at Mahogany Farms, Michigan

We were very enthused about this deal as we were being recognised in the business by two major breeders.

We decided to load the cows at Miller, South Dakota, simply because we had a little more room in the stockyards. Their men showed up a day in advance and were willing to help us get the cattle penned in the stockyards. We had to crowd our facilities to the utmost in order to leave a couple pens to sort from. The stockyards were very dry and dusty. We were ready for a long dirty day.

Bill Brittain sent Jerry Haarer as his representative and as I remember he was the new manager for Mahogany Farms. He was to do the selecting for Mahogany. He was slim and trim and appeared to be younger than he was. It seemed that at Mahogany he was always carrying feed buckets for show cattle and doing a lot of exercising and training cattle for the shows. I feared he would have trouble in selecting the cows as the decision had to be made rapidly. Lee Leachman and Myron Fuerst were to pick the cows for Ankony and they were known pros with Angus cattle.

I called the working crew together and told them how we were going to do it. We would have two empty pens - one on each side of an alley. We furnished a man for each gate to let the cows "in" or "by" as they were sorted. We would bring 20 cows in the alley. Then the 2 sorters would match to see who took first choice and the other took second, alternating like this until all 20 cows were sorted for ownership. Then we would bring 20 more cows into the alley and continue the process.

Everything started out excellent and worked better than we had hoped — trying to sort 600 cows in a small stockyard. Our biggest handicap was the dust kicked up by all the cows milling around in the very dry yards. We stopped two or three times during the day and watered the yards down. That made it real pleasant sorting instead of a miserable situation.

Our game rules were set before we started and everyone kept in line with his job. The cows handled wonderfully and showed excellent disposition which made our job of sorting much easier. Of course it was a long day and the working crew were about as tired and dirty as anyone could get.

I watched Jerry Haarer. He was alert and eager all during the process of selecting cows and I thought he did amazingly well for a boy of his age. At times since when I have seen him and we have visited about this cattle deal, he tells me about this whole story and that this was the very first time in his life that he thought he had a chance of growing up to be a man.

Jerry as of this day is the Land Management Director at Michigan State University where he manages the University Farms and properties totaling 23,000 acres in 33 counties.

On this particular shipment of cattle I decided I needed to send my top man with the cows to their destination as it was very important to further business with both of these valued customers. So I made arrangements with Cal Gadd to make the trip because he was responsible and had the know-how to handle any situation with cattle that had to travel a long distance by train.

We felt that we should send a pair of good saddle horses with the cows as they were used to horses and handled really well with saddle horses. We took two of our saddle horses that we used to drive the cattle to the stockyards and sent them with the cows. We put them in a separate section of a railroad car so they wouldn't injure any of the cows.

The train did not go any farther than the west edge of Chicago, so the cows and horses were unloaded, fed, watered and rested for 12 hours. Then the railroad company had trucks that hauled the cows and horses around the lake to the railroad that took them on to Michigan.

Cal got the cows and horses unloaded and delivered to the Farm in Michigan. The people on that end were pleased with how well the cows looked after the long train ride. They used the horses with much satisfaction and pleasure as they worked great for them in the small pastures in Michigan.

With the evaluation results from these 300 cows, Mahogany Farms realized that in order to capitalize on the improved breeding it was necessary to control the animal from "gene to steak". They developed a processed steak product made from the entire carcass. They pressed it into a strip steak shape, blast froze it and packaged it for supermarket sales.

In the late 60's Mahogany Farms decided to expand the "gene to steak" concept. One of the phases of the program was to have 20,000 to 30,000 commercial cows to raise the necessary feeder cattle. They incorporated as Premier Corporation.

Jerry Haarer, herdsman; Ray Smith, mgr; Bill Brittain, owner; Mahogany Farms, Michigan; Clayton Jennings, Hyland Angus Ranch, South Dakota, 1961 Ankony Angus sale in New York

Chapter 41

This Old House

This old house had an unbelievable story unfold inside it's walls. This young family had six children, three years of age and younger, when they moved into it. They had no running water except in the kitchen and no indoor plumbing. Every day there were dozens of diapers on the line (no disposable diapers either). They managed all the hardships with lots of laughter and a song in their hearts.

During the 1950's Ted and I were putting the Hyland Ranch together and with each ranch that we bought we either repaired, tore down or moved the buildings.

We had just bought the John Renner place north of Ree Heights, when we were contacted by a young farmer, LeRoy Ratzlaff, from south of Highmore. He was in desperate need of a different house. The house he was living in had only three rooms and his wife had just given birth to triplet girls, Yvonne, Annette and Lucille. They also had twin girls, Marilyn and Beverly, age 2, and another girl, Patty, age 3.

He thought the house would work for them as it was 18'x48' with an entry, kitchen, dining room, living room and three bedrooms. The local housemover, Wilbert Goldsmith, recommended this house as it was low and would not be to hard to relocate.

I knew it would be very difficult for LeRoy to come up with any cash so I made a deal with him for several truckloads of corn as payment for the house. He was pleased with this kind of deal.

This is LeRoy and Rena Ratzlaff's story:

> We had the house we purchased from Clayton Jennings moved to our place in November 1959. A friend of the family was remodeling their kitchen so they gave us their old cupboards. A Highmore plumber had a used hot water heater for sale which he offered for $15.00 installed, so we had hot and

1995 - This old house - home of LeRoy and Rena Ratzlaff and family for nine years

cold running water in the kitchen, when the pressure pump worked. We moved into the house in December.

We were glad to be in our new home as in January 1960, Rena gave birth to a boy, Myron. This time only one!

The house had three bedrooms, one big one in the back of the house where we had three double beds and a piano. The kids slept two in a bed and LeRoy played the piano and sang to them at bedtime. They said their prayers and went to sleep.

This large bedroom was quite cold in the winter, so LeRoy put a small heater in the corner. When we got up in the mornings we would run to the heater and huddle around it trying to stay warm while getting dressed.

LeRoy and Rena slept in a small bedroom. Myron had a bunk bed in the other bedroom. The girls took turns sharing this room with him.

We had a basement under the house which came in real handy when we raised bottle lambs. If it was too cold for them outside, we keep them in a pen in the basement. We had lots of them as there was always plenty of hands to feed them. We all got up during the night to feed our babies in the basement.

We lived in the old house for nine years. For quite a few years the clothes line was always full of diapers every day. Finally the children were taught to go out to the toilet out back or at least around to the back of the house.

During the winter of 1963, all seven of the children came down with pneumonia and whooping cough. They were sick for three months and the house was quarantined all that time. The house seemed mighty small during those long and lonely three months.

We had quite a scare when the triplets were a year and a half old. They saw a cottontail run into the cornfield (the cornfield was right next to the house) and they took off after it. We searched and searched down the rows of tall corn for them. After about three hours we finally found a bottle, then we knew we were on the right track. We found them about a half mile from the house.

We have a lot of good memories of the nine years in the old house. We never minded going out back to the outdoor toilet. We took a lot of baths in a small metal wash tub in front of the old heating stove, once a week whether we needed it or not.

Rena and LeRoy Ratzlaff and children - Patty, Yvonne, Marilyn, Beverly, Annette, Myron and Lucille (Marilyn and Beverly and twins, Yvonne, Annette and Lucille are triplets)

Most of our clothing came from the second hand store at the Stephan Indian Mission. We ate a lot of commodities that we purchased with a couple gallons of gas from some of LeRoy's Indian friends, who would stop by on their way to Highmore.

Life was simple and we cherish our memories in that old house purchased from Clayton Jennings.

Chapter 42

Texas Hunters

One of my best buddies in the Navy was Christy Williams of Houston, Texas. We spent over two years together in the South Sea Islands under tough circumstances during World War II and we became close friends.

We kept in touch after our discharge from the Navy in 1945. He came to the Hyland Angus Ranch to visit and he was so fascinated with all the pheasants that he asked if I could arrange to have a DC3 land at the Miller, South Dakota airport. If I could he would bring about a dozen friends of his, who were all industrialists from Houston, for about a week of hunting.

I said, "Bring all you like. I will arrange everything and have plenty of good hunting lined up for them."

These were all hand picked friends of Christy's and I would have to say they were probably the nicest guys I had ever met. They were all good sports and truly enjoyed the feeling of hunting pheasants. This was the start of many trips for them to South Dakota to hunt pheasants. They came each year for 10 or 12 years. They looked forward to this hunting trip as it was a real vacation for them.

I have many fond memories of these hunting trips, but it all ended tragically on the first day of hunting season in 1963 when one

1963 - Group of Texas hunters at the Hyland Angus Ranch, Melvin Fischer, guide is 2nd from right, Clayton Jennings is 5th from right

of the hunters was accidentally shot and killed just as they started their hunt.

Hunting is still good in South Dakota. This group of goose hunters easily got their limit on the Missouri River south of Highmore. Jim Bonnichsen, Bud Moser, Richard Kusser, Jerry Kolda and Jerry Koeck. December 1994

Chapter 43

Sale of Hyland Angus Ranch News Release

My brother Ted and I had always been very close, even as children. We became partners while still following in our dad's footsteps. The Jennings Brothers was a fascinating partnership that was pleasant from the very beginning. We stood together on all decisions. I truly believe no one ever had a better partner than I had in Ted Jennings.

But in 1962 both our families had children of or near college age, and we decided for all concerned it would be a good time to divide our partnership. We were in excellent financial shape. We divided all the land, cattle and equipment to both our satisfaction.

Some time after the dissolution of our partnership, Ted and his son Ron, entered into a partnershp which continues to this day.

I sold my share of the Hyland Angus Ranch and the purebred Angus cattle in 1964 to Ankony Farm of New York.

NEWS RELEASE JANUARY 1964

FAMOUS HYLAND ANGUS REGISTERED CATTLE AND RANCH SOLD TO ANKONY FARM

From: ANKONY FARM, RHINEBECK, NEW YORK

Denver, Colorado, January 12 — A significant beef cattle transaction was announced today by Lee Leachman and Allen A. Ryan, partners in Ankony Farm, Rhinebeck, New York, one of the nation's most famous Angus breeding cattle establishments, who reported the purchase of the registered cattle division of Hyland Angus Ranch, Highmore, South Dakota, from Mr. and Mrs. Clayton Jennings. The purchase included the well-known 6,300 acre ranch and the entire herd of registered Angus as well as all feed and equipment.

The firm will be known as Ankony Hyland, Inc., a corporation wholly-owned by the partners of Ankony Farm. Lester Leachman is president and Myron Fuerst is secretary- treasurer.

The Hyland ranch is one of the better known cattle operations in the West. It was founded by Clayton Jennings and his brother Ted 20 years ago. Ted will continue to operate his commercial Angus operation.

Regarding the sale Clayton Jennings said, "We are proud of the record we have made over the past 20 years at Hyland Angus Ranch with our cattle — both purebred and commercial. The infusion of Ankony's famous herd sires and females with the Hyland registered herd gives me great belief that the future potential of this breeding establishment is unlimited."

The entire staff will continue with Ankony Hyland Angus and Clayton Jennings will continue active with the ranch and registered cattle. Les Leachman commented, "In the past Ankony Farm has taken many major steps toward the improvement of beef cattle. Since more than 60% of the nation's beef cows are located in the 17 western states, we believe it extremely important to expand in the direction of the heart of the beef industry. We have highly successful units in New York and it will remain our eastern headquarters."

"We also feel sure that with the establishment of Ankony Hyland, Inc., we will have an opportunity to serve many more purebred and commercial Angus cattlemen with the correct kind of breeding stock at fair prices."

Leachman also stated, "The program of Ankony Hyland, Inc., is to combine some of the very best of the East with some of the most excellent Angus in the West. We plan to hold an annual sale at the ranch as well as having breeding stock available for private treaty sale at all times."

The major transaction was handled through the facilities of the Canning Land and Cattle Co., Staunton, Virginia.

Clayton, Ron and Ted Jennings - some of Ted and Ron's grass steers - fall of 1987

1995 - Some of the 900 steers Ron Jennings had on feed in his yards at St. Lawrence, South Dakota

Ted and Polly Jennings' son and family. Ron, Jeff, Jeanie and Laurel Jennings - 1994

PART IV
1964 - 1990

I sold the Hyland Angus Ranch to Ankony Angus Corporation of New York in 1964. I then built a retirement home on the southeast edge of Highmore, South Dakota. I moved my wife Eloise, and my three children, Charlie, Gloria and Jim into this home.

I thought I could retire at fifty years of age, as I was financially set for the rest of my life, but I was too young and too ambitious to take life easy.

I began buying and selling livestock and using the barns and corrals that I had built on my acreage near Highmore. I also was affiliated with several large cattle investment companies in this area. I handled the buying of their cattle and placement of them on maintenance.

In 1981 when all my properties were gone, except the house and after my divorce from Eloise, I put the house and all our personal property up for sale. Following the sale I moved to my present location - a small ranch on the outskirts of Highmore.

Chapter 44

My Highmore Home and Livestock Handling Facility

After selling the Hyland Angus Ranch to Ankony Angus of New York in 1964, Eloise and I decided we would buy some land near a town or city that we liked and build a new home and livestock handling facility and operate it to the extent we desired.

We started looking for a place and it seemed that we could find no area that we liked as well as Highmore. We traveled all over America. We liked a lot of places but none suited us like Highmore. This was mostly because I did not want to leave the cattle country that had been so good to me.

We bought 160 acres southeast of the Highmore city limits. We tore down the old buildings on this property, except for a granary and garage.

My home in Highmore in 1973

We built a 80x48 three bedroom home. It had a full basement with two bedrooms, a pool room, utility room and a large recreation area. We had several walk-in cedar closets in the basement for storage. Over the attached double garage was a large room that I used as an office.

In the fall of 1964 we remodeled and built onto the corrals and put in a good set of lifetime steel rod fence. We also built some outbuildings.

In 1972 we built a 48x80 steel building to house an office, inside working chutes, an inside livestock scale with a balcony for observation and bath facilities with enough space left for a deluxe hospitality room that I dreamed of finishing for the entertainment and fun of my friends and customers. My dream was to fashion a room more fantastic than any one its size anywhere including Las Vegas.

This room which became known as the "Cow Palace" was 42x34. I spent most of the time on a sawhorse, planning every move of the carpenters. The most inspiring feature to me was the hip-roof ceiling made with 18"x12" beams and cedar tongue and groove lumber. We hung large beautiful chandeliers from this ceiling. The 12' high walls were papered with wild animal print wallpaper. I had built a red horseshoe shaped bar with 12 green padded chairs.

On the east side of this room was a king-sized bed flanked on each side with smaller beds. A large fish aquarium hung on the east wall over the king-sized bed. On the west side of this room was a small kitchen and a beautiful bath with a large chandelier hanging from the ceiling.

A curved stairway led to the overhanging balcony room which was directly over the horseshoe bar. In the balcony room were six barrel chairs that fit around an octagon table used for card playing. A large fish aquarium at the far end of this room was bordered on each end with a small bed.

At the top of the curved stairway on the north side, a door opened out onto a catwalk where my customers could observe their cattle being weighed and worked in the indoor chutes. When the Cow Palace was finished I was really proud.

I feel that the many people who came and enjoyed my hospitality at the Cow Palace have been a real tribute to me and my life. The door was always open to all visitors (men, women and children) from all walks of life and all nationalities.

In the basement of my home. Arlene Vilhauer, Robert Gadd, Jake Vilhauer and Gordy Zens - the Country Roads, entertaining at one of the many get-togethers at my home

Dean Branine and Ray Sommers tending bar. Two handy men who helped at parties and get-together at my home and in Denver.

The building that housed my office, indoor livestock handling facilities and the "Cow Palace" - 1974

Clayton and Eloise Jennings at the horseshoe bar in the Cow Palace - 1974

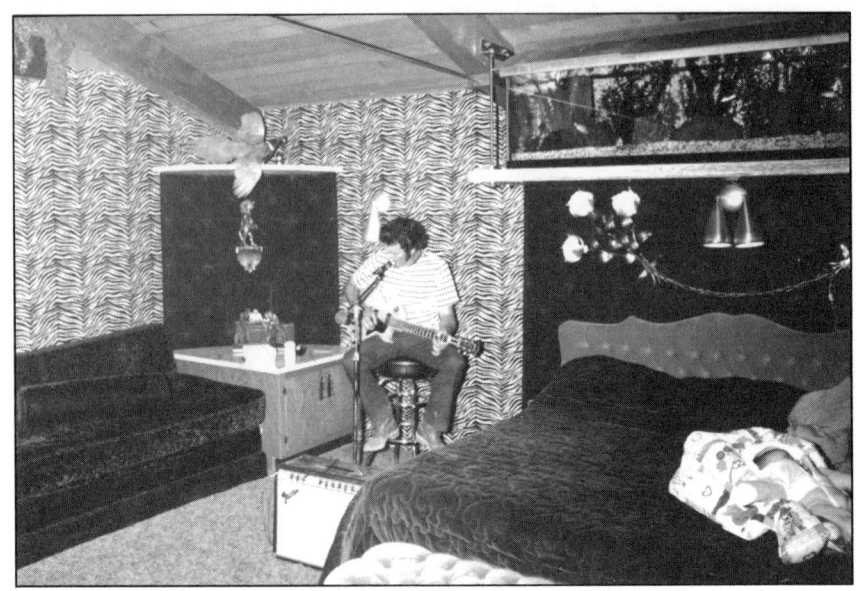

Mike Beagles entertaining in the Cow Palace. Note the aquarium over the king-sized bed - 1974

Some lady friends enjoying the balcony room in the Cow Palace - 1974

Working cattle in the indoor facilities. To the left - the scale and observation catwalk - 1974

View of our home and livestock handling facilities - Highmore in the distance

Chapter 45

A Test of Courage

My oldest son Charlie and Craig Cropsey, son of Dr. L. M. Cropsey, were both juniors and roommates at the Colorado Academy in Denver in 1968. The Academy was a four year high school for boys.

The Academy highly recommended a four day father and son rubber pontoon trip down the Green River in Utah. They sent us the information. The trip would take us from Maybelle, Colorado, on the Yampa River into Utah where we met the Green River, then through Desolation Canyon and Gray Canyon to the town of Green River, Utah, which would be the end of our journey. Doc Cropsey and I talked it over with our sons and decided that it would be a unique and possibly worthwhile adventure.

Craig Cropsey - 1968

Charlie Jennings - 1968

I packed what Charlie and I would need. We were to travel light. The Academy suggested a raincoat or rainjacket, toothpaste and toothbrush, a sleeping bag and a life jacket. We didn't need to bring any food or money. The food was all furnished and we wouldn't need any money where we were going. It was "no man's land". The cost of the trip was about $400.00 for each father and son, which we paid in advance.

I flew to Denver where I met Doc Cropsey. We picked up the boys at the Academy and drove in Doc's station wagon to Maybelle, Colorado, on the Yampa River, which was our starting point. We left Doc's station wagon at Maybelle. When the four days were over we would be delivered back to our vehicle at Maybelle by bus.

We arrived at Maybelle early in the morning. There we met the two young men, probably 30 years old, who were professionals in this type of trip. They were responsible for all our well being on this trip. We also met the other two father and son teams that would be taking this trip with us.

We loaded our gear on a 12 x 20 rubber pontoon, which was steered by rudders at the front and rear of the pontoon. We got on board. We always wore our life jackets and rain gear. The two guides took over the rudders and they worked together like one big machine. They told us about the different aspects of the river and showed us numerous hand holds to use on each side of the pontoon when the river was swift and wild. We soon found out that they were really good guys, and they were willing to answer any questions we asked.

The first day out was very beautiful and inspiring. The river was swift but relatively smooth and we did a lot of laughing and joking. I'd say the first day was really fun.

About an hour before dark we docked for the night quite a ways down river on a flat sandy beach. We were on federal land and this was a good grazing area for cattle. We could see quite a bunch of cows and calves in the distance. We helped take all the supplies ashore. After we had unloaded all the supplies we gathered some wood and got a fire started for our supper. We found plenty of firewood, as the area was thickly populated with trees. We hadn't eaten anything since morning and we were about as hungry as we could get. The guides cooked us a wonderful steak and baked potato supper on the grill. It was about the best meal any of us had ever had.

After supper when we had everything cleaned up, we sat around the campfire telling stories and jokes. We asked our guides lots of questions about the country. They told us there were lots of wild animals in the area. They said it was highly infested with bears.

After a good visit the guides said we better put the fire out and get into our sleeping bags, as we had a long day ahead of us tomorrow. I for one and most of the others didn't sleep a wink as it was so different sleeping under the stars in sleeping bags.

Very early in the morning, while it was still dark, the herd of cows and calves we had seen in the distance the night before, came down to the river without noticing us. When they came back from the river after drinking they came right to our camp. The cows spooked when they snapped some twigs on the ground. They stampeded right through our camp. There was no sleeping after the stampede, because we humans were spooked worse than the cows and calves.

Since it was almost morning and we were all up anyway we got the fire going for breakfast. We had a breakfast deluxe - hotcakes, bacon, eggs, coffee and sour dough biscuits - plenty of it as we would not eat again until supper. After breakfast we snuffed out the fire, reloaded the pontoon with all our gear and started our second day.

Our second day out was not as beautiful and inspiring as our first day. We just wanted to get off!

The river was very swift with large boulders and rapids that we had to maneuver our pontoon around. Our guides on the rudders were very good at navigating us on the right sides of the boulders. Water splashed on us. Even though we wore our raincoats all day we were soaking wet most of the time. The sun would dry us out and then we'd hit more rapids. Water sprayed on us continuously. Often we had to bail the water out of the pontoon so we wouldn't sink. We bailed with coffee cans and gallon cans. Numerous times our pontoon would stand straight in the air so high that no water supported us then we would crash into a hole in the water. That's when we discovered what the handles on the side of the pontoon were for. We went over the rapids just like a miniature roller coaster.

We were all happy when we reached our destination for the night, as we were all tired and hungry and wished the trip was over.

We landed an hour or so before dark and went through the same routine to eat. Once again it tasted like the best food we'd every had.

We didn't sit around the campfire very long that night, but the guides did have time to tell us some scary bear stories. We weren't to worried as we hadn't seen a bear yet. We were tired of being bounced around the pontoon. We were tired of being wet all the time. We all just wanted to lie down and sleep.

Doc Cropsey and I and our two sons had our sleeping bags in a circle about six feet apart so we could visit. I couldn't resist temptation after hearing the bear stories and besides I needed a good laugh and some fun. So an hour or so before daylight I quietly went over to where Doc was sleeping and grabbed him by the foot. I made bear noises as loud as I could. The noise woke up the whole camp. I kept aggressively jerking and pulling Doc's ankle and dragging him around, all the time growling like a bear. Doc was in shock beyond description! He was frantically trying to escape the bear's grasp!

This was over thirty years ago, and Doc hasn't forgiven me yet!

The whole camp was awake so we had an early breakfast and made ready for our third day on the Green River. I don't think there was anyone on the whole trip who looked forward to the third day. They just wanted off! There was no smiling, no laughing and no cracking jokes.

The river was even more snaky with more severe rapids that were 30 seconds to one minute of sheer terror. We went up, down and all around with the water continuously showering us. The canyon walls were of solid rock and so high we could only see the sun at high noon. It seemed that the walls of the canyon bent over the river below. If we could have had the chance to get out to where we came from we would have.

One of the group asked, "If I walked out of here how long would I have to walk?" The guide said, "You'll never get out alive! This is no man's land!"

Somehow we made it through the third night without any abnormal incidents. We wanted the trip to be over. There were no smiles, no laughing and no cracking jokes.

The fourth day that we were on the Green River was short and not too rough. I would say a really easy day after what we had been through on the third day out. We arrived in Green River, Utah, about noon where we were to board the bus that was to take us back to Maybelle, Colorado, where we had left Doc's station wagon.

Every day as our trip progressed we learned how wild and treacherous the river could be and we appreciated the fact that we had two such knowledgeable and capable guides. But about two weeks after our trip we heard that one of the young men who was a guide on our trip, flipped out on the rapids and was never found. If we had realized that something like this could happen we probably would have stayed home.

On land, after four days of rafting, we struggled to regain steady legs as we congratulated ourselves for the teamwork we put forth, the camaraderie, and the respect we'd learned from the water's strength!

This is without question the most challenging four days I had ever experienced in my lifetime, except maybe when I was in the Navy on the island of New Georgia constantly under the heavy fire of the Japanese!

We all came away physically stronger, mentally tougher and much more humble and with no desire to try it again!

Chapter 46

Caravelle Cattle Company

In January 1969 I received a phone call from Al McClelland of the Caravelle Cattle Company of Miami, Florida. McClelland called to tell me that Caravelle was interested in putting out a bunch of cows on a yearly maintenance basis. I had been recommended to him by several people that I could get the job done if he could get me. We talked for at least an hour in detail and his comments and desires seemed to be for real. He asked if I could fly down to their headquarters in Miami, Florida, at which time he would be in a

1995 - Ralph Myers flew Hyland Angus Ranch personnel all over America in the interest of cattle buying. We called it hedge-hopping

position to make the deal and it sounded like if it materialized it would work right along with the rest of my cattle business. Nothing tried nothing gained!

I already had commitments to look at some purebred cattle just out of Omaha, Nebraska, and Quincey, Illinois, so I chartered a four passenger single engine Cessna 206 Turbo plane with Ralph Myers as pilot to fly me on a round trip hedgehopping cattle deal. I bought a number of purebred cattle on these two stops. Then I flew on to Miami to look into the prospective cattle deal with Caravelle Cattle Company.

I recall that we hoped to get to Miami that evening but the weather turned into heavy rain and dense fog, so we landed in Jacksonville, Florida. We had to fly through the fog, rain and muck for at least half an hour before Ralph could find a hole to get down and through to the airport. I was highly concerned about landing in one piece. This was the worst flying conditions

1995 - My flying attorney, Ruben Widmayer, flew with me on many trips in case I needed legal advise

I had ever been in and I was happy to get on the ground and wait the night out. I decided right them that Ralph Myers could fly me any place any time and with full confidence.

I called McClelland and told him where we were and that we were forced to stay there all night, but we would arrive the next morning and we would call him upon our arrival at the airport in Miami.

When we arrived I called the Caravelle office. They came right out to the airport and picked us up in a big limousine with a very impressive chauffeur. When we pulled into the headquarters I could tell that we were going into a fancy high-geared operation. It didn't scare me a bit but it did alert me to what I might expect. I could see that there were numerous offices and they were as plush as I had ever seen.

The receptionist at the front desk was shockingly beautiful and pleasant. Her soft voice could melt almost any man. She led me down a wide hallway to Mr. McClelland's office. That was the first time I had ever seen him. I had only talked with him by phone two or three days prior. We shook hands and I could see he not only was a handsome man and dressed immaculately, but had personality plus and intelligence to spare.

We visited a short time and then got right down to business. He laid his program on the table to me and it seemed to fit me exactly. He told me his company would buy up to 5000 cows on a five year program. The cattle would be paid for in full as I bought them. The payments on the maintenance of the cows would be paid to the ranchers involved every thirty days and any bonuses would be paid to the ranchers when the calves were weaned. Everything would be paid through his office. The people investing in this program were all professional and big money people who were looking for a tax shelter and the capital gains program that had just come in was perfect for them. It could run on for five years or more.

I would be in charge of their cattle purchases, sales and maintenance operations. My decisions would be absolute and final and they would back me up 100%.

McClelland fully convinced me that this was a good deal for me and this really inspired me. I would not need to put up any money, but would receive a commission on every thing I bought for them, sold for them and for placing the cows on maintenance with the ranchers. I was to receive $10.00 per head on every cow that I bought and payable at delivery time. I was to receive $5.00 per head for placing these cows with various ranchers and I was to receive $10.00 per head for each cow when I sold them payable at the time of the sale. I agreed to pay my own expenses on the cattle bought and sold, but there was no risk on my part. The risk belonged to Caravelle Cattle Company. I had very little expense so the commissions were in the total of each bunch of cows I bought. This was a neat profit and clearly set. Volume was the name of the game from then on. They assured me that they were able to pay for as many cattle as I bought and as soon as I bought them. We shook hands and called it a deal. I was a commission man from then until they dispersed.

McClelland took my pilot, Ralph Myers and I out for dinner in one of the finest restaurants in Miami. He put us up in a hotel for the night and personally took care of all our expenses and took us back to the airport the next morning. We got into the air at a decent time and flew into Beloit, Wisconsin, to visit Dick Walsh and his purebred Angus operation. We flew out of Beloit the next morning and arrived back in Highmore that evening.

There were plenty of commercial cattle for sale for $250 to $300 per head. I promised Caravelle young sound bred cows. Quite a few ranchers heard of this deal and when they got to figuring that they could get up to $208 a head yearly for maintenance and bonuses, paid monthly and with no risk, they felt it was a better deal than owning the cattle themselves and taking the risk. The bankers were hovering over the entire cattle industry and money was getting harder to get to run their operations - interest was on the rise and cattle prices were stagnant and it was surely not encouraging to the cattleman.

My phone rang busy all day and half the night from ranchers wanting to know in detail about the deal. Most all of these ranchers made a deal with me, for whatever number of cows I agreed we could put with them on the maintenance basis.

After a few years, time ran out and Caravelle Cattle Company elected to sell all of the cattle. We called a dispersion sale. We had the sale on the Boots Gregg Ranch twenty-three miles south of Harrold. Lots of timber and open areas were within one hundred yards of the Missouri River. We advertised it well. We posted signs on all roads leading to the Gregg Ranch. People had no trouble getting there.

I leased an enormous tent about the size of a circus tent. We put up portable corrals and many pens. We had several top auctioneers work the sale. We got through selling cattle about dark. The volume buyer was Premier Cattle Company from Lansing, Michigan. They bought over half of the offering which made for an active sale. The prices were not too high, but modest. This was the first cattle Premier bought for a similar cattle investment deal.

After the sale Boots Gregg's daughter and her husband, Bonnie and Wayne Bartlett, invited us all up to their beautiful home on the ranch for refreshments. They offered us any kind of refreshment and a large buffet of food.

I had a lot of stress getting everything organized for the sale and I was exhausted. I recall everyone having a glorious time. I saw a nice long couch. I went over and lay down for a little rest. It felt so good. I dozed off to sleep.

Someone started massaging my back and my head. It felt so good, I just laid there moaning and groaning hoping it would go on forever. There was a lot of laughing and joking going on all over the house and I was unaware of what was happening to me. Two of Boots Gregg's granddaughters, Corrine Aasby and Pat Thorn and their aunt Bonnie Bartlett mixed up a liquid solution of red food coloring and dyed my hair. I thought I was getting a massage, but in reality I was getting my hair dyed! Finally when so many people were looking at me and laughing so hard I went to the bathroom to see what was wrong with me. It was shocking. My hair was bristled up and was no certain color. It looked pink at one time and red at another, but it was neither. It was a God awful color.

Everyone was having the laugh of a lifetime seeing me in this situation. I said, "Girls, you know I am committed to be at the First National Bank in Miller tomorrow morning with the proceeds of the sale of these cattle!"

The girls gasped and said, "Oh my God, Clayton, why didn't you tell us?" They tried and tried to get the color out by washing and washing but my hair was still PINK. The three girls apologized as if they were sincere. They had a lot of fun but I was embarrassed.

My theory - never trust any girl 100%!

The next morning I arrived at the bank on time. I walked into the president's office with my hat pulled down as far as possible. I never took it off. The minute I finished my business I got out of the bank. I noticed all the people in the bank saw my hair job and were smiling or laughing.

When I left the bank I went to the Earl Houck Barber Shop across the street and was determined to do something about this awful hair appearance of mine.

I took my hat off and Earl Houck who was a good friend of mine said, "What happened to you?" The story was too long to tell so I told him I was run over by a freight train. I told Earl to cut my hair as short as possible - teddy bear style - and not to try to remove the color because it wouldn't come out. I told him the whole story and he was so amused and laughing so hard he had to quit for a while. When he finished he gave me the mirror and I'm not sure which looked the worst - the pink hair or the teddy bear haircut! I survived but this incident is prominent in many people's minds after twenty-five years.

Chapter 47

Spring Storm Catastrophe

During the 1970's Premier Cattle Company of Lansing, Michigan, had a maintenance deal with Stanley Johnston. They ran about three hundred registered Angus cows on his ranch five miles south of Ree Heights, South Dakota. These were all valuable registered Angus cows worth from one thousand to two thousand dollars per head.

We had a severe spring snow storm that forced one bunch of 114 of these cows from the shelter of some trees adjoining a stock dam. The dam was about twenty five feet deep. When the wind changed it pushed the cows down the bank of the dam and onto the ice. The winter had been very cold so the ice on the dam was two or more feet thick. When they got about to the center of the dam, the ice caved in and they could not get out. There was ice all around them. They floundered until every one of the 114 drowned.

I called the headquarters in Michigan and told them about the catastrophe. They evidently had insurance on them as they demanded that we cut off an ear for identification for ownership and insurance purposes. Each cow was tattooed in the ears with her identification number. We had to have a licensed veterinarian do the recording of the tattoos. We used chains and cables to pull the dead cows out of the dam. Some were caught under the ice away from the hole that they had fallen through and did not surface until the ice thawed.

We contacted the rendering company to haul off all these dead cows. We expected the rendering truck every day around 4 o'clock to pick up the animals we had processed that day - pulled out of the dam, cut off an ear and recorded the tattoo numbers. It took us about two weeks and a lot of hard work to get every animal out of the dam. We were relieved when the last cow was loaded on the rendering truck.

This was the most nauseating situation with the terrible odor and sight, in the gloomiest atmosphere, I had ever experienced.

Chapter 48

Smith Ranch

Waymon Smith was working for the Production Credit Association (PCA) in Texas during the 1940's. In 1949 Mrs. J. D. Smith and son Brownie (no relation) of Rotan, Texas, acquired a loan from PCA to stock two ranches they owned in South Dakota. The PCA sent Waymon to South Dakota to make their inspection. Waymon said that when he got to South Dakota he had never seen the likes of grass and water.

Waymon Smith - May 1962 - on his way to the ranch

Waymon had a ranch leased in Texas and the lease had run out, so Mrs. J. D. Smith told him to send all his cattle in Texas to South Dakota and he could partner with her. Waymon ordered a train and he shipped all his cattle by rail from Aspermont, Texas, to Ft. Pierre, South Dakota.

After Mrs. J. D. Smith died, Waymon and Brownie were partners until 1954 when Don and Jeff, Waymon's sons, bought out Brownie's interest. Waymon, Don and Jeff bought the south ranch from Brownie. They also leased the Scottie Phillips Buffalo Ranch until it sold in 1972.

Waymon loved South Dakota but he soon learned of the hazards of ranching in this country. One such incident occurred on May 5th, 1968, when a freak spring blizzard blew out of the northwest. Smiths had a thousand steers on the Buffalo Ranch and this intense blizzard drove them from their shelter and they drifted into a stock dam and three hundred of them drowned.

Waymon used to say this about South Dakota. "It can promise you more and give you less than any place I know on earth!"

I had the opportunity to meet Waymon, Don and Jeff Smith in the early 1970's when I bought their cattle for the Premier Cattle

Jeff and Waymon Smith

Company, an investment company that I was working for.

I paid $500.00 per head for the Smiths' one thousand young top quality Angus cows. I also made a deal with them to keep the cattle on their ranch on a maintenance basis. The maintenace of $12.00 per head per month was to be paid the first of each month. And a bonus was to be paid, yearly, on a percentage of live newborn calves and a percentage of weaned calves. It was possible for them to receive about $214.00 per head per year if they met all the requirements.

Smiths' performance record was the best of all the ranchers we had in the Premier commercial cattle program. They were the only ones who received the total bonus every year for four or five years. They had a well managed ranch and they did a great job.

This proved to be a good sound move for the Smiths' as they were able to clear the debt on their land and cattle and have $200,000.00 left which they loaned back to the bank.

I had many pleasant cattle deals with the Smith Ranch over the years and I know of no more honorable men than Waymon, Don and Jeff. Their handshake always proved to be 100%.

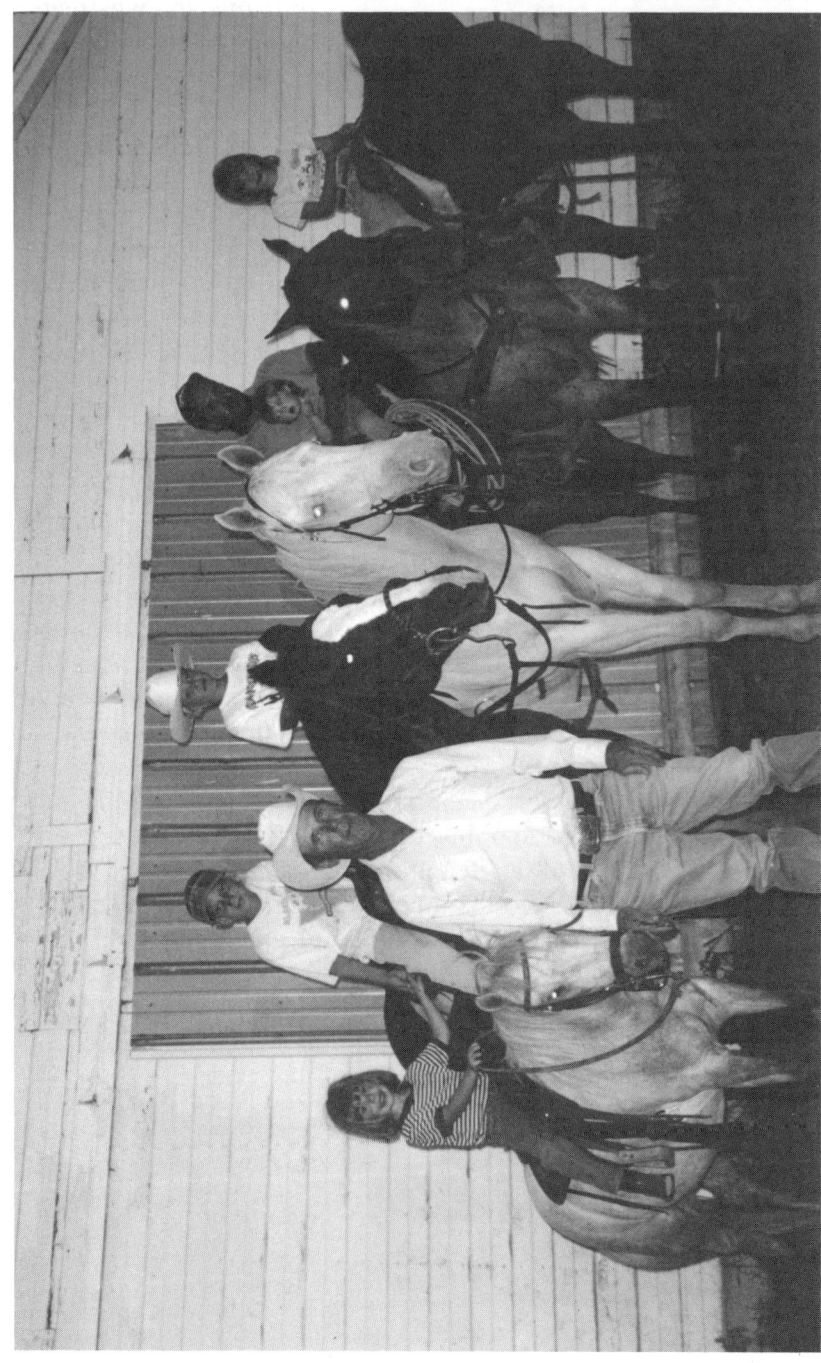

Four generations of Smiths. Don Smith, standing. Sarah Harrison, Blake Johnson, Beth Johnson, Don Lee Smith holding Hannah and Rachel Harrison

Note the Smith Cattle Co. brand on this cow. Taken on the South Ranch, Ft. Pierre, SD

Chapter 49

Who Was Pat Cowan?

I had never met Pat Cowan personally but I did know of the Cowans in the area. One night in 1967 Pat called me on the telephone. He wondered if I could do him a favor.

Pat had a big family of really young children, possibly four or five at the time. He told me that he had to move out of the house he was living in the next day. He was aware that no one was living in the Mark Durfee home just east of the salebarn in Highmore. I had owned this acreage for some time and had sold it to Ankony Farms of New York.

I told Pat I could call Myron Fuerst in New York and find out their plans for this home and let him know later that evening.

Myron was one of the big wheels with Ankony but I reached him on the first try. I had a really good conversation with him and explained the situation. He said that they would not need this home for six months or more and if I could recommend this boy, he would be willing to let him use it until they needed it. We talked about rent and Myron said if he was a friend of mine and a decent guy he would take $50.00 a month. I told him I would guarantee the rent money and take any responsibility.

This whole transaction by phone didn't take over twenty minutes. I called Pat immediately and he seemed overjoyed and thanked me profusely. Pat and his young family moved in the next day.

The next time I met Pat Cowan was some time later. I was living on the edge of Highmore where I had built a new brick home and developed a high class livestock handling facility.

Pat called me one day and asked if he could come out and talk with me for a short time. I told him I would be pleased to visit with him. If he had the time to come out then, I wasn't busy. I had an office in a large room over the double garage in my home where I spent much time.

Clayton Jennings and Pat Cowan in front of Clayton's office and cattle handling facilities - 1974

Pat Cowan and Clayton Jennings in Clayton yards, Highmore, SD with Beef Friesen bulls - 1974

Pat and I visited for quite a while and he told me what he had been doing. He had been training horses at the Sioux City, Iowa racetrack. He was only making a scant living for his young family of six or eight boys and girls. He wanted to hire me to teach him how to buy and sell all kinds of livestock. He was very humble and seemed very sincere.

We talked about all kinds of livestock and ranchers and deals that I had made that he was aware of. He thought that I was the best livestock dealer and rancher that he had ever known. In fact he gave the impression that I was a father figure to him.

I felt real good that he seemed to have unquestionable confidence in me. He insisted that he wanted to learn from me and he wanted to pay me, so I got an idea.

I said, "Pat, I won't charge you anything for helping you, but I am going to make a several day trip to the northwest corner of South Dakota and the southwest corner of North Dakota. I know numerous ranchers there and I am going to try to buy some of their cattle." I told him if he would drive part of the time, I would pay all expenses and it would not cost him a dime on this first trip and I would show and tell him about my cattle dealings. Pat was elated.

We decided to leave the next morning. This would be a good chance for he and I to get acquainted and find out more about each other. We visited day and night on the entire trip of four or five days. We bought several hundred cattle for later delivery.

I was highly impressed with Pat Cowan. He seemed to fit every occasion that came up - whether it was a business deal or just socializing.

On the way back home we had one more ranch to stop at and try to buy their cattle. I said, "You have listened and watched on every deal I've made. Now it's your turn. I want you to deal with this next rancher in accordance with the prices and weights and the quality of the cattle."

Pat was not shocked but surprised and he said, "I'll give it a try."

The rancher was a bachelor and a man of considerable age. Pat made a smooth deal and bought the cattle worth the money. He handled everything with an air of professionalism.

We headed for home and through the experience I had with Pat during the four or five days I felt he was the right kind of partner that I so desperately needed. I complimented him about his natural ability in handling people and evaluating livestock. He showed me absolutely no short comings of honesty, ability and desire.

After this trip I evaluated Pat Cowan as the most talented young man that I had met in the livestock business.

We talked at length about a partnership deal and he finally admitted that he didn't have any money to finance a business. I had sold my ranch and cattle and was in excellent financial condition and had unlimited credit at my bank. I was easily worth two and a half million in liquid assets, which included yearly payments on the ranch, many certificates of deposit in the bank and other properties of value - including a $150,000.00 paid up life insurance policy.

I volunteered that I would handle the financial end of our partnership. I had a feeling that I could help this young man prosper and also do well myself. I was so impressed with Pat Cowan in every faze of life that I didn't think he could do any wrong.

At the time I was involved in a going business that was as near a cinch financially that I had ever experienced. I was closely connected with an investment cattle company (Premier Corporation) that needed someone to buy and sell cattle for them on a volume basis. I was paid a standard commission for buying the cattle for them of $10.00 per head, another $5.00 per head for placing these cattle on maintenance with different ranches. Then I received another $10.00 a head for selling them when the time came. These investment companies were all sound and had plenty of money. They would usually run about a five year period, then disperse. They were geared for people with big incomes who needed and were looking for tax shelters.

At the peak we had about forty five or fifty thousand cows on maintenance for these livestock investors. To get the big volume of cattle we had to go to Wyoming, Nebraska, Colorado, Montana, North Dakota besides South Dakota. It took every minute of our time to keep up. It was a big project but we were making big money. These big cattle companies were at our mercy and they treated us with respect and trust.

The first month we bought a lot of cows in bunches of one thousand each but they crowded us to buy more and more cows as they had a tremendous amount of money to invest.

I offered Pat a 50/50 partnership on all profits or losses. I would handle the financial end of it and at regular intervals Pat and I would sit down and figure up our profits or losses and I would pay him 50% up to that date. We had one special book in which we both kept the records of our partnership operation. It was a solid blue, six by nine, shorthand book. The "blue book" was a concise record of each deal we made with various cattle people. Every time we completed a deal we put the facts and figures of profit or loss on a separate page. Every transaction was to be recorded in this book and our profits or losses calculated. Pat's profits were to be paid as he so desired. We kept the "blue book" in the upper chest drawer in my office over the garage that was easily accessible to either Pat or I.

After people heard that Pat and I had become partners they seemed to want to warn me about him. I would listen and say nothing simply because I didn't believe it. But there were so many people making derogatory remarks about Pat that I should have listened.

In the beginning of our partnership (C and J Cattle Co.) we spent a lot of time together planning and making our business accurate. Our business developed so big so fast that we mutually agreed to travel and do business separately. We just couldn't keep up with everything by being together.

We flew in private planes of Cecil Ice and Ralph Myers and hedge-hopped all over several of the western states. Our communication was kept up every evening by telephone by either me to Pat or Pat to me. We always talked at length about the deals he had and the deals I had and what the customers demanded. We were buying nearly all the cows that we looked at, ranging from two hundred to three hundred dollars per head. They were mostly Angus and black baldy, and mostly commercial cows. We had the responsibility of purchasing these cows plus making deals with various ranchers to keep these cows on maintenance on a yearly basis. We had more than our hands full in this operation, but we were willing to work day and night for the commissions they paid us. The more we bought the more we made without any risk - all risk was on the investment company.

The investment companies sent out representatives of their men to manage the cattle that we placed on maintenance. Herb Marks became the big overall manager for the biggest operation - the Premier Cattle Company of Lansing, Michigan. He had a crew of men with equipment and the know-how to oversee all the operation.

The program seemed to be working for everybody, but it was a fast track to keep up with. We were willing to put in the extra effort, time and stress, for the nifty bunch of profit we were compiling.

After about a month I asked Pat to come out to the office as we had a nice profit that I wanted him to share in. I had kept the "blue book" up to date to this time and his share was nearly $30,000.00, which I am sure was more money than Pat had ever gathered in his short lifetime. He was surprised and pleased at making so much money in such a short time. We thoroughly talked over our responsibility to the people who were paying our commissions and we both agreed to do everything possible to make them a success in this big venture. They trusted us to do a thorough and good job, so we always made the best deal we could when buying the cows and the best job we could of placing the cows on good ranches with sound people.

I had a list of ranchers with numbers of cattle for sale in South Dakota and Wyoming. I told Pat to go ahead and exploit these deals as best he could, but to keep in close touch with me. If I wasn't home, I would leave word where I could be reached, so we could discuss and keep our deals up to date.

Pat and I were both busy buying cows. I also kept extra busy with ranchers who wanted to take cows on maintenance. Several months had gone by and our commissions had grown big, so when Pat was home the next time I called him in to look over our up-to-date summary.

When I showed Pat the amount he had coming he was amazed and said, "Clayton, I can't take that much money, but I do need some cows." He wondered if I could give him cows in lieu of profits.

He said, "Clayton, some day I want to have one thousand black cows just like you used to have and a ranch big enough to support them."

We discussed this in detail and I told him in plain and no uncertain terms that it could be done but he would have to keep good records and I would have to report these transactions on my income tax forms to the Internal Revenue Service. I told him I didn't want to get into a messy deal with IRS and taking cattle on a basis like this would have to be reported as income. I was very emphatic when talking to Pat that he would have to keep good records of the cows that he took and their value in lieu of his profit.

I was really not in favor of this, but I said I would go along with it with the understanding that we had. We went along on this basis for a year or two making money and with Pat taking cows in lieu of profit. Then one day in the mail I got a letter from IRS of Pierre, South Dakota stating that they wanted to examine the Cowan and Jennings (C and J Cattle Co.) records for 1973 and 1974.

I called them immediately and asked when and how they would like to examine our records and that I would comply with their suggestions for a meeting, preferable in my office as it would be more convenient and more comfortable at my home.

They decided to come over to my office in Highmore to have access to all the records. They came every afternoon four days a week for several weeks. I turned the "blue book" over to them and have not seen it since. In researching I find that the IRS gave the book back to Pat as he was a full partner. That book was the key to everything in our partnership, and I doubt now that it still exists.

I received a letter from the IRS clearing my personal returns 100% and all my records were returned to me, except the "blue book" which was the most important record of all.

Shortly after, Pat received notice from the IRS that they were charging him with income tax evasion and fraud. He brought the notice to me and we talked at length about the IRS charge of tax evasion and fraud. This was the first time that I was aware that Pat betrayed me on the handshake. It was an embarrassing situation to have the word out that Cowan and Jennings were being examined by the IRS.

Finally Pat slapped his hand down on the table and said he had to get the best attorney in the State. He hired Tom Foley out of Rapid City, South Dakota, who was rated as the best criminal tax attorney in the State. Before he would even look at Pat's case he wanted $10,000.00 down. Through his attorney, Pat settled with the IRS. And as I remember Pat told me it cost $288,000.00 to the IRS and over $40,000.00 to Tom Foley and he still had to appear at St. Paul, Minnesota for fraudulent measures, of which he was acquitted.

This was a horrible mistake that Pat Cowan made by not reporting the cows he received in lieu of profit which we had talked over

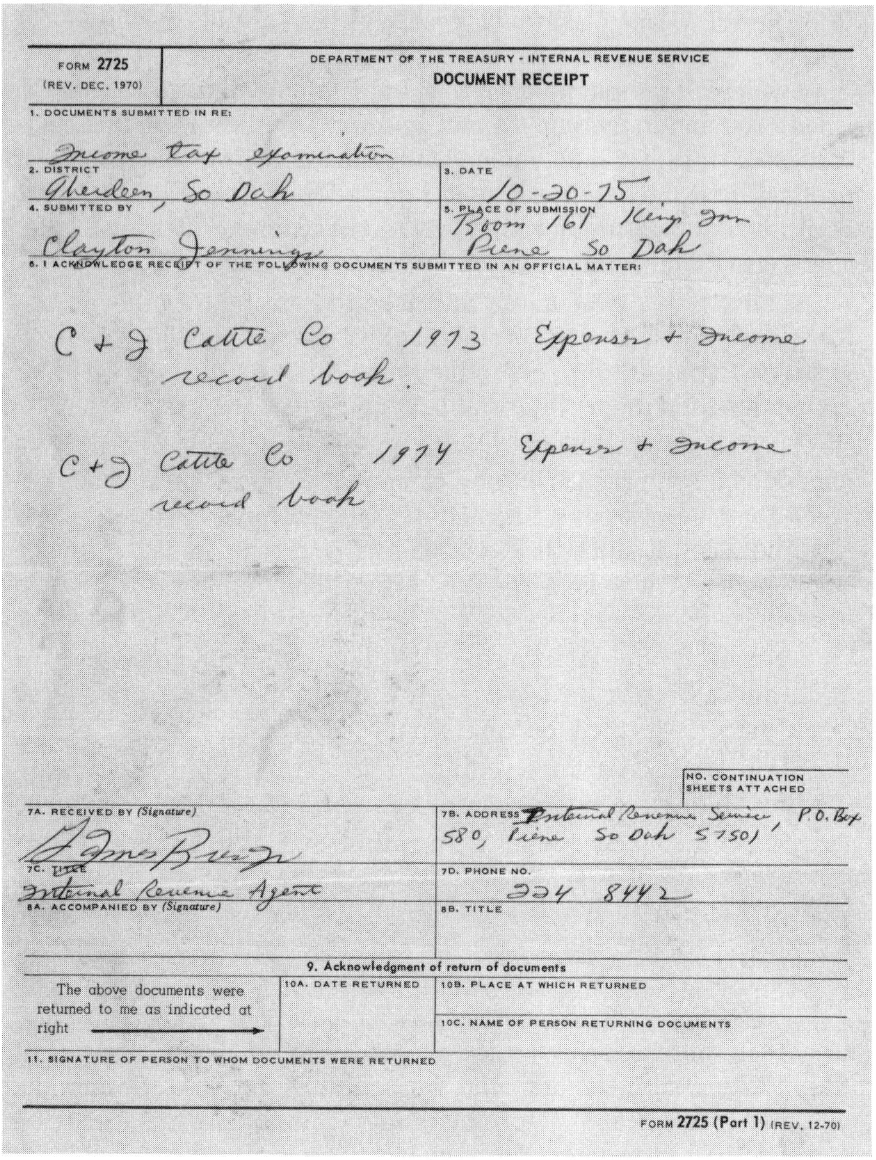

FORM 2725 (REV. DEC. 1970)	DEPARTMENT OF THE TREASURY - INTERNAL REVENUE SERVICE
	DOCUMENT RECEIPT

1. DOCUMENTS SUBMITTED IN RE: Income tax examination

2. DISTRICT: Aberdeen, So Dak

3. DATE: 10-20-75

4. SUBMITTED BY: Clayton Jennings

5. PLACE OF SUBMISSION: Room 161 Kings Inn, Pierre, So Dak

6. I ACKNOWLEDGE RECEIPT OF THE FOLLOWING DOCUMENTS SUBMITTED IN AN OFFICIAL MATTER:

C + J Cattle Co 1973 Expenses + Income record book.

C + J Cattle Co 1974 Expenses + Income record book

7A. RECEIVED BY (Signature): James Bush

7B. ADDRESS: Internal Revenue Service, P.O. Box 580, Pierre, So Dak 57501

7C. TITLE: Internal Revenue Agent

7D. PHONE NO.: 224 8442

8A. ACCOMPANIED BY (Signature):

8B. TITLE:

9. Acknowledgment of return of documents

| The above documents were returned to me as indicated at right → | 10A. DATE RETURNED | 10B. PLACE AT WHICH RETURNED |
| | | 10C. NAME OF PERSON RETURNING DOCUMENTS |

11. SIGNATURE OF PERSON TO WHOM DOCUMENTS WERE RETURNED

FORM 2725 (Part 1) (REV. 12-70)

Document Receipt from Internal Revenue Service - 1975

so thoroughly when we made the deal. This entire miscue of his had to be paid to the federal government and his attorneys - in cash.

One day at my shipping yards at Highmore, Pat came in and told me about two fellows that he had bought calves from and that they would be in that day. He said, "They are higher than hell, but I'll make it up to the Company (but he never did)." He said he had a purpose in buying the Bill Fischer and Bill Wendt calves too high. Bill Fischer had a bank in Pierre with a lot of money to loan and Bill Wendt was the head of the Production Credit Association which had all the money anyone needed. And he said he was getting ready to make a big loan with both or either of them.

There were several truckloads of calves that were at least $25.00 to $30.00 per head higher than the market making then about eight or ten thousand dollars too high. The sellers were happy and why shouldn't they be getting a price like that for their calves!

This happened one or two more years and Pat put nothing back in the Company for their overage in value. Pat's entire purpose was to get a big loan from the bank or PCA. I didn't like the strategy that Pat was using. I felt it was like a big bribe in disguise. I believe that later Pat did get his loans.

Pat became very interested in buying ranches - several of them. He would ask my opinion of what they were worth and if they were a good buy. It seemed that Pat confided in me in every deal of land or cattle and it made me feel good, but I told him to do a lot of thinking about the hazards and the glory of ranching.

He was wanting to buy land with a down payment and terms. He would negotiate the interest between eight and ten percent, which is normally too high over a long term. He thought he could buy more land this way, by putting it on a term basis. He thought land was a good investment and he was optimistic about the future.

One day after Pat had bought several ranches I asked him if he realized how totally in debt he was. He agreed that he was gambling but felt everything would work out good.

I looked at several ranches with him that he had bought. I told him that it was dangerous in the event of a downward economy and lower markets to buy too much land with too much future interest and it could eat him up in a few years. And the hazard of a severe drought would add to his risk. I told him if he bought much land on term, he had better take his best ranch and keep it clear and never borrow on it, because he might need it as a launching pad to start over if land prices went down and interest crept up. He could lose everything he had as that's the history of this country. Too much interest on too much land has proven to take a rancher out of business in a matter of a few years. The economy is the barometer of your ranch operation.

Pat kept optimistic and continued to buy land as he was making good profits on our partnership. One day Pat came into the office and wanted to visit with me about a very important ranch deal he had. He told me that his grandad, Boots Gregg, wanted to sell his ranch to him on a long-term basis with a small down payment and a low rate of interest of six percent. He also had the privilege of delaying any yearly payment in the case of a drought.

Pat was truly enthused about this ranch and I was in agreement with him. I knew the ranch well as I had bought a lot of cattle from this ranch over the years. It was a good ranch located south of Harrold, South Dakota along the Missouri River. They had always run from five hundred to six hundred cows every year, except in the drought years.

Pat didn't want to hurry the deal, but he thought he could buy it for $65.00 an acre. He wanted to know what I thought and it didn't take me long to tell him it was the best deal he had made on any land and considerably safer.

I trusted Pat Cowan, he had the use of my office in my home anytime. He could come and go as he pleased, whether I was at home or not. Since we both traveled a lot, we would be in or out of town at different times.

Then one of the most shocking episodes of my life occurred when Eloise demanded that I listen to her in regards to Pat Cowan. She had mentioned to me numerous times before that she needed to talk to me about Pat and that he was taking partnership cattle and boasting about it to her. I always turned her down and walked out of the house if she wouldn't let up on that kind of conversation. Then one night late, around ten or eleven, as I was sitting at my desk in the office, she walked up the stairs holding the Bible on her right hand with her left hand on top of the Bible.

She said, "Clayton you have got to listen to me!" And this time something told me it was important to listen to her. Tears were coming from her eyes and rolling down her cheeks. This was the first time I had seen her with tears in her eyes. I sensed that this was highly important in both our lives.

Our conversation lasted over two hours and she insisted on giving the details of the affair she and Pat had created soon after our partnership had started. She insisted on telling me every gory detail and when, why and what for of the heavy romantic period she and Pat had gone through and his continuous boasting to her of how many cows he was getting.

This shook me to my heels and I was at a loss as how to respond. The disillusionment to me was so great that I hesitated to make a decision. They both meant a lot to me and I feared I would lose them both. I felt that everything was going to explode.

Early the next morning I went over to my new office and Pat was there. He seemed quite aware that I knew our partnership had to cease NOW. So we cut off our partnership as of that day - the completion and clean-up of it would be as soon as possible.

Both Pat and Eloise gave me the same story, "We thought we were in love". Pat's infiltration of my home was unforgivable! I was starting to see through Pat Cowan and how blind I had been!

I have struggled with manic depression all my life and I declare it is the most hazardous disease of mankind. My doctors told me that my manic depression is created by stress of overworking of the mind and body. It may come on slow and it may be slower to overcome. Manic depression occurred after two horrible experiences in my life - the destruction of my partnership and the divorce from my wife. Now was the time for me to be alert and figure out what had been going on, but the depression took over. I was unable to function in any common sense manner.

When I made the partnership with Pat Cowan my net worth was over two and a half million dollars and Pat's net worth was very small with him only owning a small band of brood mares. After our partnership I wound up with less than nothing and had to take bankruptcy to exist. When Pat Cowan was killed in a plane crash in 1985 near Ft. Thompson, South Dakota he had under his control fifteen to twenty thousand acres and two thousand cows.

This story looks and sounds like an unbelievable impossibility but is exactly what happened in a span of about ten years. This is the unsolved mystery of the C. and J. Cattle Co.

My final opinion of Pat Cowan is that he was the biggest and shrewdest con-man in the history of the South Dakota livestock and land business. He was unable to handle temptation, greed or prosperity.

My biggest regret is the fact that I failed to follow my Dad's 10th commandment which he preached to me so often during my growing up years.

"Boys, don't ever get too big for your britches. Don't ever, ever take on more or bigger deals than you can keep up with. I've seen it wreck a lot of people!"

Chapter 50

Easland Limousin

In the late 1960's I had the privilege of meeting Jim Easland from DeSmet, South Dakota. He was the formulator and manufacturer of AlfaCon Feeds which he made by grinding sun-cured alfalfa hay into meal, mixing it with precise proportions of vitamins, minerals and antibotics. He pressed the mix together into pellets or into range cubes. Jim was one of the all-too-rare feed makers who would go out into the pasture or feedlot with his customers.

Jim stopped by the Hyland Angus Ranch one day as he knew I was developing a lot of breeding bulls for resale. We had a good get-acquainted visit. He said he had the best bull growing feed in the business and that I should try it. We could self-feed these bulls which would save us a lot of labor of feeding the bulls. He guaranteed that the bulls would not founder or grow long toes and they would develop hair like velvet and show a lot of vigor and vitality. I doubted this in it's entirety but I was willing to try it. I hoped it would work as I had a lot of bulls to develop. I made a deal with him to haul the feed and put in the creep feeders. I wanted the feeders kept full all the time.

The bulls did develop exactly as he said and I could see this feed was exactly what I wanted. It was a blend of #1 ground alfalfa, a little additional protein plus corn screenings, minerals and vitamins. He never did tell me exactly what all was in it, but it turned

Jim Easland, DeSmet, SD

out to be a miracle feed for the bulls. After I saw the first results I put all of our bulls on this feed. Jim hauled feed regularly to the Hyland Angus Ranch and we continued to do business with him for a number of years.

The next time I saw Jim Easland, other than casual meetings, was in Las Vegas at a big cattle show where most of the exotics of Europe were being shown. Jim and many other people were convinced that the Limousin were the cattle of the future. The bull that took everyone's eye was Prince Pompadour. He dominated the interest of most of the people at the show.

Jim was one of the leading men in the Limousin business as long as he was in the cattle business. He was prominent in all Limousin functions and had the desire to breed the best purebred Limousin cattle in the business. Jim was the most persuasive and convincing of any cattleman in the business. He developed a great herd of nearly four hundred cows.

One day in the late 1970's Jim called me and asked me if I could come down and go through his cattle with him. It would be a privilege and pleasure to work with him on a great set of Limousin cattle.

Jim told me that he had put a lot of money in this herd of cattle by keeping the tops every year and he thought he ought to take some money out of the operation as he had borrowed considerable money to get this herd developed.

Jim and I rode together in his pickup in every pasture he had. We would stop occasionally and survey the cattle. Nearly every cow had a big beautiful calf at its side. About as beautiful as any set of cattle I had seen. Then we looked at the yearling heifers and they were absolutely great.

Jim's son Roger rode with us in the pickup off and on during the day. He evidently was a partner in the cattle as he seemed to know every cow and every calf and their ancestry. I was very much impressed with his knowledge of these cattle. He was alert and personable and seemed to have a deep interest in this herd of great Limousin cattle.

When we finished looking at the cattle, Jim opened up to me. He told me he was thinking of having a sale and it had him scared, as anything can happen in a sale. He said he needed $650.00 per head on all these cattle in order to pay the bank and have a little left to go on.

Roger Easland with their Limousin bull Farfelu

Roger Easland today - paster of the Congregational United Church of Christ, Pierre, SD

I told Jim that I didn't think he would have any trouble getting that done, but of course the sale belongs to the buyers and there are a lot of elements involved in any big dispersion sale. With any sale of this magnitude there is always a big risk.

Jim kept doubting that they would bring $650.00 average, so I offered him a proposition or insurance. If the cattle brought under $650.00 I would pay him half of the shortage and if they brought more than the $650.00 he would pay me half of that figure. I'd also guarantee to have more buyers there than he could dream of, as I knew most of the purebred Limousin breeders. He agreed that this might be feasible for both of us and we shook hands on the deal.

Jim made up his sale plans and sent me a copy of everything I needed. I hired my son Charlie and daughter Gloria to help in soliciting buyers from a big area - all of South Dakota, parts of North Dakota, Nebraska and Iowa. Both Gloria and Charlie had a car. I gave them a list of the Limousin breeders and sent them on their separate ways to advise the breeders of the many great cattle that would be selling. I followed up with a lot of telephone calls to every Limousin breeder I knew.

When sale day arrived everybody was buzzing about the Easland dispersal sale. The sale was held at the Bales Continental Commission Company in Huron, South Dakota, which holds a lot of people, but it was overflowing with eager buyers ready to buy. Roger was in charge of the handling of the cattle - feeding and grooming for the sale. He had them in excellent condition and had every one of them looking their best when the sale started.

It was a glorious event and Jim Easland was aware that I got many good buyers to the sale. My daughter even bought fifteen or twenty cows for her own use. I would have to rate this as one of the smoothest big time sales of any breed. Jim was beaming with joy. He said he would call me in a few days and have me meet him in Huron to settle up.

In a few days he called me to meet him at The Plains in Huron. When we met he said, "I don't have all the receipts together yet and besides that my banker thinks I'm paying you too much!"

We roughed it out and it looked like Jim owed me something over $60,000. I volunteered to say, "Jim, just give me a check for $50,000. and we'll call it square!" He did just that. His word of honor was the same as a handshake and Jim Easland did everything we mutually agreed upon.

I came back to Highmore and issued checks to Gloria and Charlie for their share of the deal. Gloria and Charlie had a great experience in the livestock business and all that goes with it.

Chapter 51

Harvey Tschetter

One of my most interesting customers to buy from, sell to or trade with is Harvey Tschetter of Hitchcock, South Dakota. We have been doing business since 1980. Our deals, mostly bulls, have always been fun and educational.

Harvey farms heavy and does a really thorough job of raising purebred Charolois cattle and feeding cattle.

Harvey is equally sharp whether he is buying, selling or trading cattle of any kind. He has been willing to take the necessary risks that go along with weather and economic conditions of South Dakota.

Harvey is blessed with a most pleasant personality and everyone likes him on the first meeting. He enjoys socializing and is the life of the party.

Harvey is a big name in a big territory in this country.

Clayton Jennings, Dick Mott of Maher, Colorado, Harvey Tschetter and Harvey's son - 1995

Harvey Tschetter and Jake Boomsma in front of a 6.2 million bushel high moisture ground ear corn pile at Lloyd Waller's feed yard, Holdridge, Nebraska

Chapter 52

Peterson Farms

Peterson Farms of Hitchcock, South Dakota, is a highly successful father (Oscar) and three sons (Brad, Danny and Lenny) partnership that I have had the privilege of doing business with for fifteen years. I have bought bulls from them, sold bulls to them and traded bulls with them. Dealing with them each and every time has been a pleasure.

Peterson Farms is one of the smoothest big operations I have known. They own 100 quarters of land, 60 of which is farmed with wheat, corn, beans, sunflowers and millet. They have the biggest and best farming equipment available. This spring they added a twenty four row corn and bean planter. The other 40 quarters are grassland. Their cowherd consists of 900 cows, mostly Angus. They finish out to market many of the off-spring.

It is always a challenge to deal with Oscar and his boys as it is a mystery who will get the best of the deal until the very end.

Oscar Peterson and Clayton Jennings - 1995 - making another deal

Clayton Jennings, Lenny, Oscar, Danny and Brad Peterson - 1995

Chapter 53

The Last of 12,000

In 1962 when Ted and I divided the Jennings Brothers partnership, Ted kept all the commercial cows and I kept all the registered cows. Every cow on the commercial ranch was home-raised and every one of them was bred by Jennings Brothers Hyland Angus Ranch and practically all were bred by artificial insemination by the world's most renown bulls.

In the 1980's the First Bank Stock Corporation of Minneapolis was in the process of eliminating many of their large agricultural loans in this area of the country, which resulted in the sale of many cattle.

In March 1986 at the Miller Livestock Sales Company the complete dispersal of one of the greatest commercial cow herds in the United States occurred. Three thousand bred cows sold on March 21st and fifteen hundred bred heifers (some with calves at side), one thousand heifer calves and one hundred bulls sold on March 22.

Every one of Ted Jennings' Hyland Angus Ranch commercial cows sold at this sale with many of them staying in South Dakota or going to surrounding states. Quite a number of these cows are still producing and everyone declares that they are the greatest cows they ever owned.

The price from $500.00 to $575.00 will live with the buyers forever, as by the following fall the pairs brought double the cost. They were the products of artificial insemination by the greatest Angus bulls of the time. This sale put a lot of the ranchers in the Angus business in the top echelon.

Carol and I attended the sale at the Miller salebarn. We found a seat on the crowded bleachers. There were buyers from surrounding states and from all over South Dakota. By sale time it was standing room only. We hadn't planned to buy any cattle, but we got caught up in the frenzy of the crowd and the bidding.

Carol and I loved the cattle coming through the ring and they sounded so reasonable. Carol wanted to buy some so I told her to

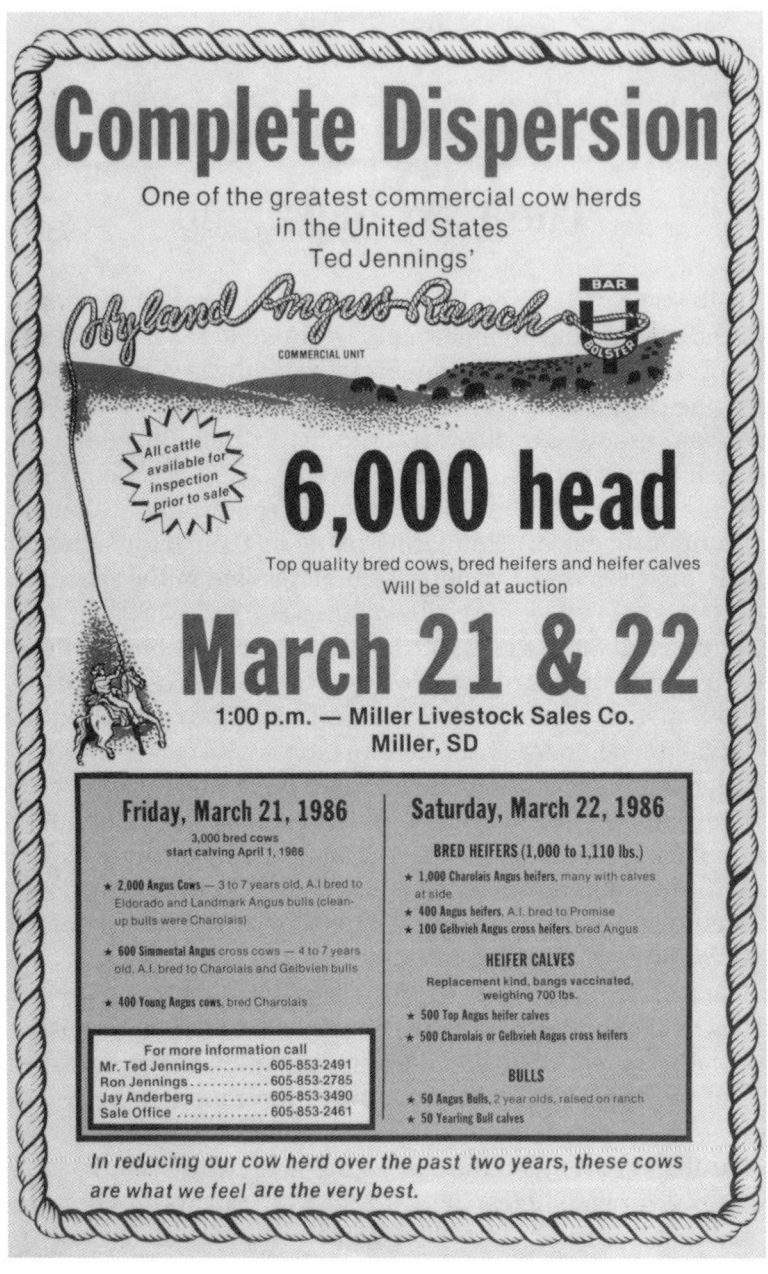

Sale Bill of Hyland Angus Dispersal - 1986

just raise her hand until she got them bought. We bought all first-calf heifers. Some of them had calved during the night and some while the sale was going on. The calves were too young to bring into the ring, so they were sold sight unseen. That was good enough for us as we knew the cattle. They cost us $505.00 a pair.

We found someone to haul the heifers and calves to my place on the edge of Highmore. We put them in the barn for the night. We were so proud of our purchases.

The next morning when Carol arrived for work we went out to the barn to check them. We saw a horrible sight. All the calves were sick with the 24-hour scours. Some were lying flat and some that weren't quite so sick were curled up, but they all needed attention right away.

When Carol saw them she fell apart. She started crying and yelled and screamed at me.

"Clayton, do something, you've got to do something before they all die. I wish we would have never bought them!"

I got her calmed down and had her go to the house and call the vet. He came right out and surveyed the situation. He gave us his thinking on the sick calves and was ready to treat them immediately, which he did. We lost only one calf and the rest healed up in a few days.

We put the cows and calves on pasture shortly after and they all grew and gained beautifully and afforded us real pride. We had them running in a pasture along Highway 14 and several people stopped and wanted to buy them.

In November Jake Vilhauer who farmed near Highmore came by to compliment us on the cattle. He said he wanted to buy the wet heifers when we weaned the calves. Since he liked them so well, we sold them to him for $620.00 to be delivered the next week as we had consigned the calves to the Highmore salebarn. The calves averaged $565.00 and weighed a little over 600 pounds, which is some weight for a heifer's calf. We doubled our invested money in less than seven months.

Almost all the ranchers who bought cattle in Ted's sale had similar results and it set a pattern for those who had courage to buy the good ones. It has been almost ten years ago and many of the buyers remind me of the cows they bought and say to me, "The only mistake we made was we didn't buy enough of them!"

That sale was one of the bargain deals of the era.

Just before the Hyland Angus Dispersal sale - Ted and Clayton Jennings at the Miller Sale Barn with some of Ted's cows in the background - 3-22-1986

My small ranch on the eastern edge of Highmore, South Dakota

Don't Quit

When things go wrong as they sometimes will,
And the road you're trudging seems all up hill.
When funds are low and debts are high,
And you have to smile, but you want to cry.
When care is pressing you down a bit,
Rest, if you must, but don't you quit.
Life is queer with its twists and turns,
As everyone of us sometimes learns.
And many a failure turns about,
When he might have won had he stuck it out.
Don't give up though the pace seems slow—
You may succeed with another blow,
Success is failure turned inside out—
The silver tint of the clouds of doubt,
And you never can tell how close you are,
It may be near when it seems so far,
So stick to the fight when you're hardest hit—
It's when things seem worst that you mustn't quit.

—Author Unknown

PART V
1990 - The Present

Carol had been my constant companion and helper for over ten years prior to our marriage. Then on May 30th, 1990, we were married at the Chapel in the Hills, Rapid City, South Dakota.

She has made the house on our small ranch near Highmore a very comfortable home. We are enjoying life immensely.

In 1993 we published my first book "HANDSHAKE, Code of the West". The acceptance and beautiful comments from all over America have been unbelievable and highly rewarding.

Our life today is very pleasant and worthwhile. We love our little ranch and have the desire to make this our home for always.

Chapter 54

My Wife Carol - Her Story

Clayton and Carol Jennings May 22, 1990. After their wedding at the Chapel in the Hills, Rapid City, South Dakota

Clayton and I were married in the Chapel in the Hills, Rapid City, South Dakota, on May 23, 1990. I met Clayton in 1979 after his daughter, Gloria, insisted that we should meet. I went to work for him soon after as he had hip replacement surgery and needed someone to drive him on his cattle buying trips and anyplace else he needed to go. We did not marry for 11 years, but I was his constant companion and work partner.

I had two young children at home and I wanted to wait for them to be on their own before I married. I always felt "there's enough time for me after the children are grown". I still believe that even though it is very difficult raising children in a single parent family.

Carol Wurts in front of the Wurts home - 1935

My name is Carol Ann Wurts Jennings. My life began in drought plagued 1934 at a maternity home in Highmore, South Dakota, on the hottest recorded May 30th in history. I can't imagine anyone wanting to have another mouth to feed during the great depression of the 1930's.

My parents, Vernon and Goldie Wurts, were very poor, like everyone else in South Dakota during the "Dirty Thirties". They had very little in the way of material things, but they had each other and lots of dreams of the future together. When they were married in 1931 Dad owned a small farm in Eagle Township southwest of Highmore, so he had a few possessions, but not much. He had an old kitchen table and one chair. He told Mom that she could have the chair to sit on and he would use an apple box for a chair. When I was born, my older brother Dale was sleeping in the baby bed, so Mom made me a bed on the floor behind the

Vernon and Goldie Wurts - 1971 - the farm where I grew up

stove. I don't know how long I slept on the floor, but however long it was it sure didn't hurt me any.

My folks had to have been really brave and have lots of faith in the future, as there was very little money and few jobs available for anyone. Dad worked for the WPA, a federal program that built many township roads, city streets, sidewalks and many of the stock dams in the area. He was paid a wage of $39.90 a month. Sometimes Dad furnished his own team of horses, thus receiving a little higher wage. This was better than nothing. It kept food on the table and gave the men of the community the opportunity to accomplish something. Many people left South Dakota during these hard times but the strong stayed. Dad always said he was too poor to leave, but I know better. He loved South Dakota and did not want to live anywhere else. I'm happy we stayed. I, too, love South Dakota and would not want to live anywhere else.

My grandmother, Sophia Ringer, homesteaded six miles south of Highmore in 1889. My dad was born on this homestead in 1899 and lived there all during his youth. Dad moved his family, my mom, my two brothers and me, to this farm in 1938 and that is where I grew up. Dad was diversified. He always had a few cattle, sheep and hogs. He raised oats, rye and corn for feed. The land is still in the family and it is owned and operated by my younger brother, Roger and his wife Linda.

I attended country school in a one room schoolhouse the first eight years of my education. The schoolhouse was located in our pasture near Highway 47 about one half mile from our house. The school had one teacher with one or two pupils in all the grades from first thru eighth.

We had a small white and black terrier dog named Skippy that went to school with us every day. We tried to keep him home. Mom would keep him in the house until we were out of sight (we walked every day). Then she would let him outside and he would head across the pasture the half mile to the school. When we realized it was impossible to keep him home, unless we tied him up, we took him with us every morning. Skippy was really good at school. When the teacher rang the bell for classes to begin he would run into the schoolhouse and lay on the floor. He would either sleep or just listen until the teacher rang the bell for recess, then he would jump up and head for the door. He knew it was time to go outside and play. On cold winter days, my brothers and I would have to take turns carrying him under our coats so he wouldn't freeze. He was a short-haired house dog and couldn't stand too much cold.

Aunt Mary and Uncle Ben, my dad's aunt and uncle, lived on a farm a half mile west of our farm. They were very special people and we visited them often and Skippy always went with us. Skippy would even go visit Aunt Mary almost every afternoon even if none of the family went. In those days we didn't have a telephone, so when Mom had something important to tell Aunt Mary she would tie a note around Skippy's neck and he would trot down the road taking her the note. She would tie her reply around his neck and

Carol Wurts and Skippy - 1945

he'd head for home bringing the answer back to Mom. He was very dependable. He seemed to know what we expected of him.

As I was growing up on the farm there were always chores to do, both in the house and outside. I liked the outside chores the best. My two brothers and I took turns doing whatever had to be done. We didn't get paid for doing the chores. We just knew they had to be done. This one day it was my turn to slop the hogs. After the cows were milked and we had separated the cream from the milk, I was to take the separated milk that we did not need at the house to the sows in two large milk buckets. We had a dozen or so big sows in a large yard about thirty or forty yards south of the house. We fed them in a long wooden trough. The sows always rooted the trough around when they ate and it was usually out in the middle of the yard instead of near the woven wire fence. I was carrying a bucket of milk in each hand and as I neared the pig yard I hoped that the trough would be near the fence so I could just reach over the fence and pour the milk in, but it wasn't. It was in the center of the yard. Let me tell you that sows are mean old critters and they will root anything out of their way to get to the feed. But I was in luck or so I thought! As I approached the fence I could see the sows were all asleep in some weeds at the far side of the yard. I thought I could quietly set the buckets of milk over the fence, climb over myself and get to the trough before the sows heard me. But I was wrong. They heard me as soon as I set the buckets down on the ground and here they came right at me on a dead run. I picked up the two buckets of milk and was running as fast as I could. Before I reached the trough, the sows and I collided. They were on a dead run and they hit me full force. I was knocked down, the milk buckets flew into the air with milk flying in every direction. The milk flew all over me. The old sows were slurping up the milk as fast as they could. They didn't care that they were stepping on me and rooting me around. When I finally was able to get up, I was covered with milk and dirt from the pig yard. I was a mess and I was fighting mad, I headed for the house telling everyone that I was never again going to feed those sows! My two brothers and Mom and Dad just stood there and laughed at me. They thought it was hilarious. I didn't, but now I can see the humor in it.

One summer when I was about thirteen, Mom had a plan to teach my brothers and me the value of a dollar. We always milked cows as the cream money was what mother used to buy our groceries every week. We didn't own any milk strain cows, so we milked the Herefords. She made us the following deal. She would pay us $1.00 a week for every cow we milked twice a day all summer. If we made the deal we had to stick with it, no stopping in the middle of the summer because we were tired of milking. I liked the idea and I decided I would milk three cows which would make me $3.00 a week. By fall I would have lots of money, more than I had ever had, maybe $60.00. I could buy everything I needed for school. I started right away the next morning. No matter what, it was every morning and every evening. If something came up that I wanted to do I had to arrange it so I could get the milking done first. I remember how I hated it when the flies were bad (we would spray but it didn't seem to do much good). The cows would stomp their feet or switch their tails to keep the flies from biting. They would either kick me off my one legged milk stool and spill my milk or hit me in the face with their manure covered tails. Before I finished milking I would have manure in my eyes, mouth and hair. What a mess! I kept my part of the bargain. Mom did too. She paid me the $3.00 each week. When we went to town on Saturday night I would go to the movie (if it was a western), buy some candy to take home for the week, and I would have an ice cream cone. All this would probably cost me twenty five or thirty cents. The rest I saved until fall and I was able to buy my school clothes and school supplies. I felt good that I had earned the money and I was able to buy what I needed.

I have a very fond memory of milking time. We always had lots of barn cats on the farm. They lived in the barn and survived by hunting and catching mice and birds to eat. We also gave them a pan of milk every morning and evening when we were in the barn doing the milking. While we were milking they would always sit in a semi-circle near the rear of the cow that was being milked. They knew that we would give them a squirt of milk every so often. When the squirt of milk from the cows teat came towards them they would all sit on their hind legs with their mouths open. We would squirt milk into the mouths of all of them sitting in the semi-circle. What a sight - all those cats sitting up on their haunches with their mouths wide open waiting for the squirt to reach them! I can still see them to this day!

We always had pail-fed calves off the cows that we milked. One year we had two that my younger brother and I were very fond of. One was a heifer that we named "Airin" because she was always

Roger and Carol Wurts riding Airin, the milk cow. In the distance - Smokey, the buckskin horse Carol got for 8th grade graduation and the neighbor's horse that Carol broke to ride sticking her tongue out. We said she was airing her tongue. We also had a steer calf that we called "Burro". We played with them from the time they were born until they were grown. We could catch them anywhere in the pasture and we could ride both of them. We kept Airin as a milk cow and she was a good one. My Dad sold his steers as two year olds and when the cattle buyer came to the farm and bought the steers Burro was in the group. When I heard that Dad had sold Burro I cried and cried. I didn't want him to sell my pet. Dad said, "Get that steer over the hill in the pasture when they come to pick up the steers. We will keep him another year." That's what I did. I rode him over the hill in the pasture, but when he was a three year old Dad said he had to go. I didn't say anything this time, as I knew Dad had lost money on him as it was.

I remember that the Easter bunny always came to our house. We never had Easter baskets when I was a child. My brothers and I would take Mother's bread pans and fill them with hay and set them by the front door. On Easter morning we found that the Easter bunny had come by and left us lots of treats in the bread pans.

When I met Clayton he told everyone that I hadn't been out of the county and he was about right! I went to work at the First State Bank in Highmore right out of high school and was there fifteen years. After I had graduated from high school the bank president came out to the farm and offered me a job. My dad said, "You take that job, its a good one." I had wanted to attend college, but Mom was in the hospital in Rochester, Minnesota, having back surgery and working at the bank was a great opportunity. Everyone considered a bank job as the best job available during the 1950's. My starting salary was $165.00 a month.

I remember my first paycheck, which was for two weeks work. It was about $70.00 and as soon as I got it I headed right across the street to the Tomter Drug Store and bought a Kodak camera for $9.95. Having a camera had always been a desire of mine. I love taking pictures and I believe that since Clayton's book "HANDSHAKE, Code of the West" was published in 1993 I have taken over 1000 pictures and he is in every one of them!

After working for the bank for fifteen years and being married for almost that many years, my husband and I wanted a family. We were unable to have children of our own so we adopted a girl and a boy. Lisa Marie came to live with us in 1967 and Joel Matthew in 1969. I am truly blessed to have two such wonderful children. I was

Carol and Clayton Jennings at the Navy reunion in San Diego, California - 1994

forced to give up my job at the bank as it was their policy not to employ a pregnant woman or a woman with children. A policy that has no place in the work-world today. Thank goodness!

My life changed considerably in 1979 after I met the Clayton Jennings family. First I got to know Clayton's daughter Gloria and she kept insisting that I meet her dad. He and I were both going through divorces at the time. Finally I consented to meeting him and I am truly grateful to Gloria for feeling so strongly that her dad and I would make a great team.

Clayton has exposed me to a world I never dreamed I would ever experience. I am thankful that I have had the opportunity to grow and to broaden my horizons through my association with him. He is very knowledgeable about and well-known in the livestock industry. I have met Clayton's friends and business associates, of which there are many, from coast to coast and from Canada to Old Mexico and they all tell of his honesty and integrity in the many business dealings they have had with him.

In October 1994 Clayton and I had the opportunity to attend the 50 year reunion of his old Navy buddies in San Diego. What admiration and respect they all have for Clayton! I came home feeling that I was married to the most admired and most loved man in the world! And I believe I am!

Thank you Clayton for being who you are!

Clayton Jennings - San Diego Harbor - 1994 - while attending his Navy reunion

Chapter 55

To Laugh Often and Love Much

TO LAUGH OFTEN AND LOVE MUCH;

TO WIN THE RESPECT OF INTELLIGENT PERSONS & THE AFFECTION OF CHILDREN;

TO EARN THE APPROBATION OF HONEST CRITICS & ENDURE THE BETRAYAL OF FALSE FRIENDS;

TO APPRECIATE BEAUTY;

TO FIND THE BEST IN OTHERS;

TO GIVE OF ONE'S SELF;
TO LEAVE THE WORLD A BIT BETTER; WHETHER

BY A HEALTHY CHILD, A GARDEN PATCH OR A REDEEMED SOCIAL CONDITION;

TO HAVE PLAYED & LAUGHED WITH ENTHUSIASM & SUNG WITH EXULTATION;

TO KNOW EVEN ONE LIFE HAS BREATHED EASIER BECAUSE YOU HAVE LIVED;

THIS IS TO HAVE SUCCEEDED.

Ralph Waldo Emerson

Chapter 56

Everything I Hold Dear

by Gloria Jennings Holdman

Everything I hold dear in life has been influenced by my father, Clayton Jennings. The development of my values and priorities comes not so much through his words but rather his actions. His integrity and strength of character through adversity continue to be "high water" marks for me to aspire towards.

On a recent visit home, I read through the volumes of letters Dad and Carol have received in response to his first book "Handshake, Code of the West". I was pleased to know he is held in such high regard by so many people from all walks of life, not only for his contributions to the livestock business but for his personal influence on their lives, too.

The words of Ralph Waldo Emerson have inspired me in the telling of this story.

TO LAUGH OFTEN AND LOVE MUCH;

The value of a good sense of humor, especially about himself, has been a mainstay in Dad's life. Few things have given him more pleasure than making someone laugh, whether it be by telling a new joke, a story on himself, or hosting a party for friends where laughter and frivolity always prevailed.

Loving humor always plays a great role in our family interaction, but I remember a time when it backfired on Dad. From a early age, my younger brother Jim was quite the gardener. When he was about 5 years old, he insisted on planting a watermelon patch, although we tried to explain that the Highmore growing season wouldn't allow for much of a crop. Every morning when Jim woke up, he would run out in his pajamas to check on his watermelon progress. On the way home from a trip to Sioux Falls, Dad and Eloise decided to stop in Forestburg to buy a trunk full of watermelons. Late that night, armed with a flashlight, they carefully placed the melons on Jim's vines. At breakfast the next morning, they clued me in on the practical joke. We anxiously awaited Jim's reaction. Venturing into the garden, Jim screamed for us to come out and see his "overnight success." It was only then we realized we would have to tell him the truth. It took a few days, but he finally forgave us.

TO WIN THE RESPECT OF INTELLIGENT PERSONS & THE AFFECTION OF CHILDREN; TO EARN THE APPROBATION OF HONEST CRITICS & ENDURE THE BETRAYAL OF FALSE FRIENDS;

Dad instilled the value of respect in us at a very early age. We knew it wasn't automatic. We had to earn respect. Having the respect of his family and peers has been a driving force throughout his life. His leadership and achievements have guaranteed him a place in the minds and hearts of many.

Children were always made to feel included and special — whether they were his own, nieces and nephews, or sons and daughters of the people who worked his ranches. His efforts were never a search for affection and admiration (although that was the end result) but rather to help them in the growing up process. Now as adults, many look back with wonderful memories of him.

Dad values independence and responsibility, his vision always focused even when he stumbles on his journey. Although he has surely met a false friend or two along the way, he never talks much about them.

TO APPRECIATE BEAUTY;

It has been said that beauty is in the eye of the beholder. Dads knows the value of beauty and what he likes and doesn't like. The barns and fences were always painted, and you would have been hard pressed to find a piece of trash or junk on one of his ranches. His eye as a judge of "beauty" in cattle is legendary.

When Dad began "outfitting" the "Cow Palace" some questioned his taste in decorating. As always, he remained true to himself and his vision. On one of his buying trips to Denver, I visited an aquarium distributor with him. Shortly after arriving, we discovered the distributor was a wholesaler, and I was ready to leave and look for a retailer. Within minutes, Dad not only had the gentleman agreeing to sell to him but to personally deliver and install his new custom-built aquariums in South Dakota. Of course, Dad wanted salt water fish because they came in such beautiful, exotic colors and designs. He didn't mind their high maintenance. I can remember those fish giving him a lot of pleasure...just feeding them was a kind of spiritual experience for him.

TO FIND THE BEST IN OTHERS;

Loyalty to his family and friends is of utmost importance to Dad. His encouragement and support have given more than a few people just what they needed to succeed, both personally and professionally.

Dad is one of the most non-judgemental humans I know. And, I should know since I have given him more than enough opportunities to question my character (of course, in my younger and wilder days). One of my most memorable times was a trip to Minneapolis for a Minnesota Twins game. My friend Carol (now my friend and stepmother) went along on the trip with Dad, my little brother Jim, one of his friends and me. When we got to Bloomington Stadium (always arriving early for batting practice), I asked Dad for the tickets for Carol and me and told him we would meet him inside. We took what was meant to be a brief detour through the Marriott Hotel bar next to the stadium. Well, one thing led to another and one Scotch led to another. We met a most interesting man from Scotland, and I had a fascinating conversation with him. At least that's how Carol describes the afternoon. I have very little memory of the adventure. I do, however, remember arriving at the game somewhere in the 8th inning much to the dismay of Dad and Jim. Dad wasn't upset about us being disorderly. He just couldn't understand how anyone would miss a baseball game!

TO GIVE OF ONE'S SELF; TO LEAVE THE WORLD A BIT BETTER; WHETHER BY A HEALTHY CHILD, A GARDEN PATCH OR A REDEEMED SOCIAL CONDITION;

Dad's generosity of spirit is well-known throughout his circle of friends and acquaintances. He values friendship second only to his family. The values of hard work, sustained effort and honesty are paramount in his business relationships. Dad was not a regular church-goer, although he contributed financially. His "church" was on the prairie where he spent most Sunday mornings. I often wondered if he didn't feel closer to God out there than I did sitting in the church pew. He always taught me, "Leave a place better than you found it!" and he certainly has done that many times over his life.

TO HAVE PLAYED & LAUGHED WITH ENTHUSIASM & SUNG WITH EXULTATION;

The values of play, recreation and competition are high on Dad's list. Being a successful high school athlete, he developed a winning attitude which he passed on to others. His love of competitive sports remains one of his few distractions from the cattle business.

During my sophomore year in high school, I enjoyed a certain amount of success on the track field as a sprinter and relay runner. Dad was standing at the end of every finish line I crossed that year, even having to charter a plane one day to make my track meet.

In 1969 Dad took us all to the Rose Bowl in California. I can remember him saying that everyone should go to the Rose Bowl at least once in their life. That year, O. J. Simpson was a senior playing for the University of Southern Cal. USC was defeated 27-16 by Ohio State in spite of an 80-yard touchdown runback by Simpson. After the game, Dad asked if I wanted to meet Simpson. Women weren't allowed in locker rooms in those days, but I had very short hair and kind of looked like a boy. To this day, I don't know for sure how he managed to get me into the locker room, although I believe it had something to do with money - probably a lot of it! I met O. J. in front of his locker and shook his hand. It was quite an experience for a young girl with stars in her eyes. O. J. went on to become the #1 NFL draft that next year going to Buffalo, and you know the rest of the story.

TO KNOW EVEN ONE LIFE HAS BREATHED EASIER BECAUSE YOU HAVE LIVED;

Through the value of Dad's commitment to his family and community of friends, I believe innumerable lives have breathed easier because he has lived. I know I have. From the top of the heap to the bottom, his dedication to me has been unwavering. When I was named "Miss Holiday" in 1970, the love and pride in his tearful eyes were greater than I had ever seen. Just a few short years later, when he had to rescue me from an abusive relationship in California, his devotion to me remained unchanged. As I struggle with alcoholism and drug addition, he never gave up on me. And as I now celebrate ten-plus years of sobriety, he celebrates with me.

THIS IS TO HAVE SUCCEEDED

Chapter 57

To My Dad

by Gloria Jennings Holdman

BEING A DAD IS LIKE BEING A BOXING TRAINER...

In the dressing room before the match, the trainer speaks to his fighter of courage and victory. He gives hope and confidence. If he has any doubts at all, he keeps them to himself—never letting them show.

As they walk together to the ring, the trainer exudes confidence and pride. At ringside, he helps his fighter through the ropes, places a stool for him, and gives last-minute instructions. He whispers of courage and victory.

When the fight begins, the trainer shouts directions and encouragement. He cheers and jumps with delight as his fighter lands a good punch. He strains for his words of support to be heard over the crowd noise when the punch comes from the other fighter. He yells of courage and victory.

When the bell rings to end the round, the fighter goes back to his corner to be refreshed, cared for, and uplifted. The trainer hands him a towel and water as the fighter rests on the stool. He repairs his cuts, rubs his neck, and pats him on the back. He talks of courage and victory.

And when it's over - win or lose - the trainer helps his fighter out of the ring and back to the dressing room. There, he either celebrates the accomplishment or helps put the pieces back together again. Either way, he speaks of courage and victory.

THANK YOU FOR ALWAYS BEING IN MY CORNER.

Chapter 58

Impressions

by Dale Christensen

I met Clayton Jennings in 1987 after meeting my soon-to-be wife (I married Carol's daughter Lisa), so in the past 8 years I have gotten to know him as a good friend and as Grandpa Clayt.

I, like most people in the livestock business, have been intrigued by the stories told about Clayton, Ted and the Hyland Angus Ranch, but when they are told by Clayton it brings a life to them. Through his eyes and his voice you could sense the feeling each event had on him just as it did when it happened.

The thing that impressed me most about Clayton is the way he is around people. Anybody who knows him, also knows he enjoys attention and thrives in the spotlight, but in a way to never make the other party feel threatened. Almost always he makes them feel better about themselves or life in general. It seems as if he has a clever remark or nice compliment on the tip of his tongue that either makes you feel better or makes you sit back and think. I believe this is one of the reasons once you have met Clayton Jennings you will never forget him.

The lives of the Jennings Brothers reads like a fairy tale and in a way have become legends, but most of all to me and others, they are proof that with hard work, a little luck, and good friends the American dream or your dream can come true.

Clayton, I thank you for the stories I've heard and the stories we've made and most of all, "I'm proud to claim you as my family and my friend!"

Sincerely,
/s/ Dale

Chapter 59

What More Do I Need?

I have experienced 82 years of life in this world and it has been highly rewarding and beautiful. Yet I know what sadness is; what disappointment is; what losing is; what depression is; what grief is; and what gloom and doom is.

I am grateful and proud to have three children, Charles, Gloria and her husband Andy, Jim and his wife Kim, who have established their place in life, and I shall always cherish and remember their growing up days.

I am equally grateful and proud of Carol's children, Lisa, her husband Dale and grandchildren, Laycee and Logan, Joe and his wife Vicki and grandson, Blayne.

I have always had a great need and desire for friends. Friends have been a very big part of my life. Now I realize that over 90% of my old friends are gone, so I lean on the younger generations.

One of the most wonderful things ever to happen to me was meeting Carol, my wife. Our togetherness has given us a bond and dedication that only a few find. I must say that the years with Carol have been the most beautiful of my life. She's lovely, she's unselfish, she's kind, she's understanding, she's savvy, she's giving, she's delightful, she's exciting and a shrewd business woman. She is my everything.

When Carol and I first met, I was in the toughest and worst stretch of my life — both physically and financially.

The Pat Cowan era is over. The Cowan and Jennings partnership is over and we survived.

The bankruptcy is over and we survived.

Two separate hip replacement operations are over and we survived.

Manic depression is over and we survived.

I want it to be known that Carol was everything in my survival.

Carol and I now live in a very comfortable small home on a small ranch near Highmore. We have a multitude of friends near and far. We are enjoying life.
WHAT MORE DO I NEED!!!

Index

A

Aasby, Corrine, 259
Airin, 302
AlfaCon Feeds, 278
Algona, Iowa, 90
Allis Chalmers, 65
Amazon River, 213
Amherst, Colorado, 218
Anderberg, Jay, 47
Andes Mountains, 215
Angus, 94, 95, 111, 138, 140, 143, 144, 173, 188, 203, 208, 218, 238, 239, 286
  Ankony Angus Corporation, 93, 208, 218, 226, 238, 239, 243, 244
Ankony Hyland, 239
Anthrax, 40, 41, 42
Argentina, 208
Army Corps of Engineers, 57
Artificial Insemination, 93, 95, 170, 172, 173, 175, 177, 178, 179, 219
Aspermont, Texas, 262
Avenda 9 de Julio, 213

B

Bales Continential Commission Company, 282
Bartlett, Wayne and Bonnie, 259
Behrens, Bob, 177
Belgium, 22
Bell Boy, 95
Beloit, Wisconsin, 258
Bennett, Colorado, 219
Berkeley, California, 42
Beverly Hills, California, 202
Beyeler, Max, 175
Big Bend Dam, 179
Billings, Montana, 198
Black Cats, 192
Black Hills, 94, 182
Blackjack, 147, 150
Blair, Jim 175, 179, 180

Bogota, Columbia, 215
Bones, 61, 79
Boone County, Iowa, 1, 17, 24
Boone, Iowa, 1, 19, 24, 26
Branine, Dean, 193
Brazil, 209
Brittain, William L., 217, 218, 226, 228
Broken Bow, Nebraska, 173, 175
Brooklyn Supreme, 24
Brown Hotel, 35, 63, 66
Brucellosis, 40
Buenos Aires, Argentina, 208, 209, 213
Buffalo, New York, 313
Buffalo, Wyoming, 219
Burro, 302

C

Cahalan, Art, 75, 77
California, 201
Canada, 22, 206, 306
Canning, Dave, 188
Caracas, Venezuela, 209
Caravelle Cattle Company, 255, 256, 257, 258
Cary, Illinois, 173
Cassady, 28
Cayou, O. J., 33
Cedar Rapids, Iowa, 1, 22
Cessna 205 Turbo, 256
Chamberlain, South Dakota, 66, 67
Champion Angus Steer, 150
Chapel In The Hills, 295, 297
Charolois, 218, 283
Cheyenne River, 69
Chicago and Northwestern Railroad, 94
Chicago International, 147, 177
Chicago, Illinois, 93, 140, 147, 229
Christensen, Dale, 315, 316
Christensen, Laycee, 316
Christensen, Lisa, 315, 316
Christensen, Logan, 316

Collins, Wilkie, 219
Colorado Academy, 251, 252
Colorado State University, 219
Colt's Neck, New Jersey, 173
Conner, Argyl, 147
Cook Ranch, 86, 88, 89
Cosmopoliton Hotel, 207
Cottonwood, South Dakota, 53
Cow Palace, 245, 310
Cowan & Jennings Cattle Company (C & J), 271, 273, 316
Cowan, Pat, 266, 269, 270, 271, 272, 273, 274, 275, 276, 277, 316
Cropsey, Craig, 251, 252
Cropsey, L. M. "Doc", 138, 169, 170, 172, 173, 217, 218, 219, 251, 252, 254, 255
Crownover, William, 22
Curtiss Candy Farms, 172, 173
Cutter Laboratories, 42

D

Dale's Tavern, 164
Danekas, Jim, 145
Danekas, Walter, 143, 144, 145, 147
Davis, Vern 177
Dawson, Glenn, 191, 192
Democratic Party, 61
Denver, Colorado, 150, 177, 188, 217, 218, 226, 238, 311
DeSmet, South Dakota, 278
DesMoines River, 30
DesMoines, Iowa, 33
Desolation Canyon, 251
Dinklage Yards, 37
Dinklage, Louis, 36, 39
Dor Macs Bardoliermere 24, 218
Double Diamond Ranch, 218
Drake Field House, 33
Drayson, Jim, 169, 177
Drybread, Wilbur, 173
Duroc Reds, 59
Dwyer, Eloise, 93, 207

E

Eagle Butte, South Dakota, 69
Eagle Pass Ranch, 159
Eagle Township, 297
Easland, Jim, 278, 280, 282
Easland, Roger, 280, 282
Elgin, Illinois, 173
Elkins, Milt, 36

Elm Creek, 45, 195
Emerson, Ralph Waldo, 308
Emirau, 75

F

Farceur, 20, 22, 24, 26
Farrell, Bill & Chet, 175
First Bank Stock Corporation, 289
First National Bank, 14, 154, 259
First State Bank, 304
Fischer Bros. Merchantile, 71
Fischer Brothers, 36
Fischer, Antone, 71
Fischer, Bill, 275
Fish, Dorothy
Fogelman, Ralph, 24
Foley, Tom, 273
Forestburg, South Dakota, 309
France, 22
Frances, 191, 192, 193
Fratzke, Bob, 179
Ft. Dodge Serum Company, 58, 59
Ft. Dodge, Iowa, 59
Ft. Pierre, South Dakota, 36, 37, 38, 66, 67, 69, 71, 89, 262
Ft. Thompson, South Dakota, 277
Fuerst, Myron, 145, 218, 228, 239, 266
Fulscher, Max, 218

G

Gabriel, Gary, 65
Gadd, Calvin, 141, 198, 199, 201, 202, 229
Gann Valley, South Dakota, 40, 47
Gerlach, John, 65
German, 29
Goldsmith, Wilbert, 231
Good, Grant, 20, 22, 24
Good, Mabel, 24
Good, Paul, 217
Governor, 61
Grand Central Station, 169
Grand Champion, 150, 172
Grand River Angus Farms, 218
Grand River, 69
Grandpa Clayt, 315
Great Falls, Montana, 167, 197, 198, 199, 202
Greek God, 11
Green River, 251, 254
Gregg Ranch, 258, 259
Gregg, Boots, 259, 276

Grey Canyon, 251
Grizzly Ranch, 218
Guinness Book of World Records, 24

B

Haarer, Jerry, 219, 228, 229
Haeh, Ramona, 198, 199, 200, 201, 202, 203, 206, 207
Hahn, Bud, 178
Hahn, Elinor, 178
Hahn, Mike, 193
Hamilton, Missouri, 147
Hammer, Dr. Armond, 170, 173
Hampshire, 54, 56, 58, 59
Hand County, 93
Handshake: Code of the West, 295, 304, 309
Harlowtown, Montana, 198
Harrold, South Dakota, 276
Hartland, Ed, 36, 37, 38
Hasart, Linda, 182
Hastings, Nebraska, 218
Hazzard, Phil, 169
Hedman Bros., 36
Hereford, 37, 38, 39, 40, 45, 47, 54, 56, 188, 218, 302
Highmore, South Dakota, 14, 93, 94, 164, 175, 208, 243, 244, 291, 295, 297, 299, 316
Highway 14, 67, 156, 291
Highway 47, 299
Hitchcock, South Dakota, 283
Hoagie, Ansgar, 36
Hoffman, Jack, 172
Hoffman, Karl, 172
Hollywood, California, 203
Hoover Ball and Bearing, 218
Houck Barber Shop, 260
Houcks, 61
Houston, Texas, 235
Howard, Kenneth "Duff", 50, 52, 53
Humboldt County, Iowa, 12
Huron, South Dakota, 89
Hyde County, 93
Hyland Marshall, 170

I

Ice Flying Service, 202
Ice, Cecil, 202, 271
Ida Grove, Iowa, 172
Internal Revenue Service, 272, 273

International Beef Breeders, 180, 218, 219, 226
Iowa State Legislature, 24
Iowa State Track Meet, 33
Iquito, Peru, 213

J

Jacksonville, Florida, 256
Japanese, 35, 75, 255
Jennings Bros., 14, 16, 36, 63, 93, 155, 164, 175, 238, 289, 315
Jennings, Carol, 169, 289, 291, 295, 297, 309, 311, 316, 317
Jennings, Charles Clayton, 93, 191, 192, 203, 207243, 251, 252, 282, 283, 316
Jennings, Charles, 1, 2, 5, 7, 9, 10, 11, 12, 13, 14, 16, 18, 26
Jennings, Dorothy, 182
Jennings, Eloise, 208, 209, 210, 213, 215, 216, 243, 244, 276, 277, 309
Jennings, Gloria, 93, 182, 191, 193, 203, 207, 243, 282, 283, 297, 306, 309, 314, 316
Jennings, James Ted, 93, 243, 309, 310, 311, 316
Jennings, Margaret, 1, 2
Jennings, Mary, 1, 2, 3, 4, 5, 10
Jennings, Nadine, 1, 2
Jennings, Ron, 182
Jennings, Ted, 1, 2, 3, 4, 9, 10, 11, 12, 13, 14, 32, 33, 35, 58, 61, 63, 79, 93, 154, 155, 156, 170, 172, 175, 182, 218, 219, 231, 239, 289, 291, 315
Jennings, W. O., 1
John Day, Oregon, 75
Johnson, Dave, 167
Johnson, Tommy, 38
Johnston, Frances, 191
Johnston, Stanley, 191

K

Keller Bros., 175
Kindles, 65
Kiowa County, Oklahoma, 138
Kissler, Dan and Harold, 219
Knippling Hat Brand Ranch, 40, 42, 45, 47, 48, 50, 61
Knippling, Clayton, 47, 50
Knippling, Don, 47, 50
Knippling, Jerald, 47, 50
Knippling, Joe, 40, 47, 48, 50

Knippling, John, 40, 47
Knippling, Lambert, 40, 47
Knox, Dr., 36
Kohlhaas, Matt, 28, 29, 30
Krick, Jimmy, 175
Krick, Terry, 181
Krog, Lowell, 181, 182
Krueger, Bill, 36

L

Lansing, Michigan, 259, 260, 271
LasVegas, Nevada, 245, 280
Law, Barbara, 159
Leachman, Jim, 178
Leachman, Lee, 208, 213, 218, 228
Leachman, Les, 218, 239
Lettau, Blayne, 316
Lettau, Lisa Marie, 304
Lettau, Vicki, 316
Lettau, Joel Matthew, 304, 316
Lewistown, Montana, 198
Limousin, 280, 282
Little Black Joe, 154
Livermore, Iowa, 1, 12, 26, 28, 30, 32, 35, 38, 50
Longmont, Colorado, 219

M

Magness, Jim, 35, 56, 59, 61, 63
Mahogany Farms, 217, 218, 219, 226, 229
Malibu Beach, 206
Marriott Hotel, 311
Marsden, Kathleen, 159
May, Millie, 140
May, Ralph, 138, 140, 141, 142, 170
May, Wilbur, 218
Maybelle, Colorado, 251, 252, 255
McClelland, Al, 255
McCorkle, J. B., 145
McIlravy, A. R."Mac", 52
McLaughlin, South Dakota, 69
Meadow Lane Farms, 218
Mexico City, 215, 216
Mexico, 206, 217, 306
Meyer, Alfred "Rawhide", 63, 65, 66, 67, 68, 69, 71, 75
Miami, Florida, 209, 255
Michigan State University, 138, 229
Miller City Council, 61
Miller Livestock Auction, 47, 63, 67, 68, 289

Miller, South Dakota, 14, 16, 35, 66, 67, 89, 90, 111, 145, 154, 169, 175, 209, 228, 235, 259
Minneapolis, 289, 311
Minnesota Twins, 311
Miss Holiday, 313
Missouri River, 45, 54, 57, 58, 66, 226, 258, 276
Mitzy-Bitzys, 79
Moreau River, 69
Morrison & Quirk, 219
Morrison, Kenneth, 218
Myers, Dick, 177
Myers, Ralph, 256, 258, 271

N

National Western Stock Show, 150, 177, 188, 207, 208, 218
Navy, 35, 40, 61, 75, 235, 255, 306
New Georgia, 50, 75, 255
New Jersey, 172, 173
New York, 93, 226, 243
Newman, Marlene, 208
NFL, 313
Norman, Roy, 36
Northern Illinois Breeding Co-op, 173, 180, 218

O

Oahe Dam, 57
Oakdale Farms, 57
Ogden, Iowa, 20,
Ohio State, 202, 312
Olson, June, 195, 196
Olson, Roy, 195
Omaha, Nebraska, 256
Omega Farms, 218
Oregon State University, 71
Oregon, 202
Osborn's 167

P

Palo Alto, California, 219
Parlin, David, 162, 167
Parlin, Harold, 162, 164, 165, 167, 169, 175, 178
Parlin, Larry, 162, 167
Parlin, Phyllis, 162, 167, 178
Pasadena, California, 202, 206
Paterno, Carl, 218
Pearl Harbor, 35, 75
Pender, Bill, 184, 186

Penn State University, 219
Penney and James Farm, 147, 150
Penney, J. C., 147, 150
Peterson Farms, 286
Peterson, Brad, 286
Peterson, Danny, 286
Peterson, Lenny, 286
Peterson, Oscar, 286
Petry, Nick, 218
Philip 73 Bar, 52
Philip, South Dakota, 52, 53, 69
Phillips Buffalo Ranch 262
Pierre, South Dakota, 35, 54, 57, 58, 209
Pitman, Wanda, 219
Premier Corporation, 229, 259, 260, 262, 270, 271
Prince Eric, 170
Prince Pompadour, 280
Production Credit Corporation, 261, 275
Prosser, J. J. "Bud", 219
Purdum, Nebraska, 175
Purdy, Herman, 219
Purdy, Robert, 219
Pykiet, Clayton Dean, 193
Pykiet, Karol, 193

B
Quincey, Illinois, 256
Quirk, John, Sr., 218

R
Raona Bardolier 158, 145
Raona Farms, 169, 217, 218
Rapid City, South Dakota, 273, 295, 297
Ratzlaff, Annette, 231
Ratzlaff, Beverly, 231
Ratzlaff, LeRoy and Rena, 231, 233, 235
Ratzlaff, Lucille, 231
Ratzlaff, Marilyn, 231
Ratzlaff, Myron, 233
Ratzlaff, Patty, 231
Ratzlaff, Yvonne, 231
Raymond, South Dakota, 143
Red Bank, New Jersey, 170, 173
Redfield, South Dakota, 89
Ree Heights, South Dakota, 86, 88, 93, 94, 156, 175, 182, 191, 231, 260
Renner, John, 231

Reno, Nevada, 219
Reserve Grand Champion Steer of all Breeds, 150
Reserve Grand Champion, 150
Rhinebeck, New York, 208, 238
Rhodes Brothers, 36
Ringer, Sophia, 299
Rio de Janeiro, Brazil, 209
Ristau, Hank, 26, 27
Robinson, Nadine, 203
Rochester, Minnesota, 304
Rose and McCrea, 143
Rose Bowl, 202, 206, 312
Rosemores, 65
Roseth Ranch, 36
Ross, Dick, 179
Rotan, Texas, 261
Roundup, Montana, 198

S
Sacramento, California, 201, 202
Samuelson, Martin, 36
San Diego, California, 75, 306
San Francisco World's Fair, 24
Sandkamp, Otto, 156
Sao Paulo, Brazil, 209, 210
Scotland, 311
Seattle, Washington, 75
Shadow Isle, 170, 172, 173
Simmons, Cliff, 218
Simmons, Steve, 218
Simpson, O. J., 312, 313
Sioux City, Iowa Racetrack, 269
Sioux Falls, South Dakota, 309
Skippy, 299
Smith Ranch, 263
Smith, Brownie, 261
Smith, Don, 262, 263
Smith, Jeff, 262, 263
Smith, Mrs. J. D., 261, 262
Smith, Ray, 169, 170, 217, 218
Smith, Virg, 90
Smith, Waymon, 261, 262, 263
Smithers, Mrs. Irene, 203
Sonnenshein, Earl, 69
South America, 208, 217
South Dakota State Fair, 147
South Dakota, 1, 35, 42, 45, 48, 50, 52, 54, 61, 66, 86, 94, 144, 154, 177, 186, 217, 261, 262
Spencer, Cliff, 197, 198
St. Paul, Minnesota, 273

Steers, Buck, 158
Steers, Tom, 182
Stephan Indian Mission, 235
Stoesser, Alex, 36
Suhn, Dale, 159
Suhn, Ernest, Jr., 156, 158, 175, 177, 179, 180
Suhn, Jerry, 158, 159
Suhn, Loretta, 156, 159
Suhn, Vern, 158, 159, 180
Sutton Brothers, 54, 56, 57, 58, 59, 61
Sutton, Edwin, 54
Sutton, James, 54
Sutton, John, 54
Syntex Pharmaceutical Firm, 219

T
Texas, 261, 262
Thorn, Pat, 259
Tomter Drug Store, 304
Trichomonosis, 170, 172
Trinkle, 177
Tschetter, Harvey, 283

U
U. S. Forest Service, 71
United States, 22, 61, 206, 289
University of Southern California, 312
Utah, 251

V
Valentine, Nebraska, 141, 143, 175
Van Wert, Ohio, 217
VanDervoort, Phil, 178
VanDervoort, Rand, 169, 170, 172, 173, 175, 177, 180, 182, 218
Vilhauer, Jake, 291
Vogler, Raymond, 19, 20, 24

W
Walden County, 218
Walsh, Dick, 258
Waterloo Boy, 10
Watkins, 4
Wendt, Bill, 275
White River, 68, 69
Wilbur's Feed and Seed Store, 153, 154, 209
Wilbur, Charlie, 153, 154, 155
Williams, Christy, 235
Williams, Ralph, 177
Williamston, Michigan, 218
Wilson and Company, 138
Wilson Packing Co., 1
Wisner, Nebraska, 36, 37
World's Grand Champion, 22
WPA, 298
Wurts, Dale, 297, 301
Wurts, Goldie, 297, 298, 299, 301, 302, 304
Wurts, Roger and Linda, 299, 301
Wurts, Vernon, 297, 298, 299, 301, 302, 304

XYZ
Yampa River, 251, 252